ARCHITECTURAL RENDERING IN WASH

BY

H. VAN BUREN MAGONIGLE, F.A.I.A.

ARCHITECT

GOLD MEDALLIST OF THE ARCHITECTURAL LEAGUE OF NEW YORK, ROTCH TRAV-
ELLING SCHOLAR, FELLOW OF THE AMERICAN INSTITUTE OF ARCHITECTS,
PAST-PRESIDENT OF THE ASSOCIATION OF THE ALUMNI OF THE
AMERICAN ACADEMY IN ROME, PAST-PRESIDENT OF THE
ARCHITECTURAL LEAGUE OF NEW YORK.

WITH A PREFACE

BY

THOMAS R. KIMBALL, F.A.I.A.

PAST-PRESIDENT OF THE AMERICAN INSTITUTE OF ARCHITECTS

NEW YORK
CHARLES SCRIBNER'S SONS
1921

THE SCRIBNER PRESS

PREFACE

Opinion has proclaimed that a preface should introduce the author to his audience. I should add—and prepare that audience for the work itself. "Architectural Rendering in Wash" presents its author in the diverse capacities of architect, draftsman, painter, and writer. Incidentally, it suggests other qualifications of this many-sided personality. It presents its subject from the view-points of architect and draftsman, and harmonizes them. It solves a host of difficult problems and answers many trying questions. It is the architectural draftsman who will be the greatest beneficiary, who will find his work has been made easier and his output improved by the acquisition of this new and engaging text book and authority. The architect will benefit in that his work will be better presented, and possibly he may, himself, be better able to appreciate what architectural presentation means. Posterity will come in for a great acquisition in that through this work there will be recorded what otherwise might one day join the "lost arts," for architectural rendering is to-day at its zenith, indisputably an art in itself, and a great one. I foresee for this book a widespread and lasting influence for the betterment of artistic appreciation, architectural draftsmanship, and last, but not least, architecture itself; and I commend it to all whose interests embrace these subjects, and to that great group of discerning men and women, the public— on whom by the very nature of things—the future of all art must depend.

Thos. R. Kimball, F. A. I. A.

Omaha, Nebraska.

CONTENTS

CHAPTER   PAGE

I. THE PRELIMINARY STEPS 3

II. RENDERING 31

III. QUARTER-, HALF-, OR THREE-QUARTER-COLOR . . 83

IV. RENDERING SECTIONS 93

V. RENDERING DETAIL DRAWING 94

VI. RENDERING PLANS 100

VII. THE PROPERTIES OF PIGMENTS 116

VIII. FREE COLOR AND FREE SKETCHING 133

INDEX 145

ILLUSTRATIONS

The Library of Columbia University, Drawn by Jules Guérin
Frontispiece

PLATE				FACING PAGE
1	Rendered by Otto R. Eggers	12
2	Rendered by the Author	22
–	Diagram of Building Assumed to be Rendered, Drawn by Oliver Reagan	34
3	Rendered by Birch Burdette Long	42
4	" " the Author	66
–	Diagram of Typical Cornice Shadow, Drawn by Oliver Reagan	68
5	Rendered by the Author	70
6	" " the Author	80
7	" " Bellows, Ripley, Clapp and Faelten . .	82
8	" " the Author	84
9	" " the Author	88
10	" " Paul Philippe Cret	94
11	" " the Author	96
12	" " G. Redon	98
13	" " Paul Philippe Cret	100
14	" " G. Ancelet	104
15	" " Leon Chifflot	112
16	" " Frank Hazell	120
17	" " Hubert G. Ripley	130
18	" " Jules Guérin	134
19	" " Hubert G. Ripley	136
20	" " the Author	138
21	" " Otto R. Eggers	140
22	" " Ernest Peixotto	142

FOREWORD

Genius has been defined as the capacity for taking infinite pains. It takes infinite pains to make a beautiful rendered drawing. The conclusion is irresistible—one has but to make a beautiful rendered drawing and behold! A genius. Or, one need but take infinite pains and the genius and the drawing are produced by one and the same process. This modest manual is a guide to the process. With the information given here, the addition of some brains, a little temperament, a vast deal of patience (or ardor under restraint), a modicum of vision and as much imagination as obtainable from the ancestral tree, any one may arrive.

This book is devoted principally to the rendering of geometrical drawings—elevations, sections, plans and details—what may be called formal or academic rendering. It is not a general treatise upon painting in water color, although there is an indefinite middle ground between the formal and the free into which we must make an occasional excursion and a considerable body of information upon rendering in full color and sketching will be found here. But it is with the aristocrat of architectural rendering, formal rendering in India Ink, we shall deal principally, for several reasons, chief among them being that academic rendering may be reduced to a method and a formula. A definite recipe may be given, a program laid out. Without a definite method, a carefully thought-out series of steps to take, an academic rendering in India Ink is foredoomed to failure. But in free work in water color, rapid sketching on white or toned paper and architectural rendering in full color, while there must, of course, be method, much depends upon the temperament of the individual, the personal tricks of handling which stamp his work with his style, the way of seeing and the method of attack; and since every one has different systems it is an impossibility to crystallize them into formulæ —as well as being a crime. The most that can be done for free work is to give a few hints and let it go at that. For art may be learned, or apprehended, but it cannot be taught. The most one can do or should do is to say, "*I* do it in this way. But you must do it your way—when you know how!" Before a man's skill and knowledge have developed he must follow some man or some method or lose himself in a maze of mistakes. Later he may blaze a trail for himself.

It is a great temptation to a novice to use all the colors there are, in any sort of rendering and on one drawing. He likes to use color and forgets that this is not the last drawing he will make in the course of his life and that it is hardly fair to the future ones to use up the rainbow so early in the day. It is the same as in design—he forgets that if his luck holds he will design many a building and that it isn't necessary, it is even quite distinctly undesirable, to put everything he knows about into one design. A decent reticence is to be observed in this as in other things in life—one doesn't go about telling all one knows, all at once.

Every student seems to want to render geometrical drawings in full color whether the work has to be done at night or not, or whether the author of the given outrage knows how to handle even one color, let alone the full rainbow. This is a great pity. For the most distinguished architectural drawing is always the monotone drawing. The method of representing a building in elevation rather than in perspective is a convention, and the more closely one adheres to a convention in its rendition the more harmonious the relation between the fact and its presentation. The moment the third dimension appears in a drawing, as it does in a perspective, the convention need no longer be respected and the aim changes and becomes an approximation of reality. The truth is that the average student-rendering in full color is intended to make a noise which will cover up some shortcoming or kill its neighbors. If a value is wrong, it may be blamed upon night work in artificial light. But in a monotone drawing there is not a chance. If a value is wrong it is wrong. I therefore urge students in or out of school to practise rendering in India Ink before going on to the use of color. It is one of the few forms of self-denial with a tangible reward.

Another reason for treating principally of formal rendering is that the average American student of Architecture is altogether too fond of short cuts, is apt to be superficial and is impatient of the solid things that lie at the foundation of his art. Among these solid things is a kind and method of study and presentation of architectural design which really trains his eye. The French, trained for generations in the effort to teach art, know this; and the Grand Prix men in their first year at the Villa Medici—do what? Make careful studies of the orders in India Ink as a preparation for the work of the years to follow and as a sort of purge and corrective of the kind of work they have been doing at the *Ecole des Beaux 'Arts*. Large Frenchmen with beards do this, quite unashamed. And some of those who, at the School, indulged in the most untamed vagaries of design, pace soberly and with apparent willingness in the restraining bonds of academic rendering.

The rigid discipline it enforces in the judgment of values and tones, the training the eye gets in discerning the difference, let us say, between two whites in which there is scarcely a breath of difference near by but which at a distance count with a totally different force, the exercise the hand gets in perfecting a technique, are all of inestimable value. Why so much emphasis upon draughtsmanship, upon presentation? Because by means of drawings the eye is trained to appreciate values in the distribution of light and shade and color—and it is with light and shade and color the architect deals all his life. And how is he to effect the distribution of his light and shade and color without making drawings which accurately express it, first? How can he make drawings which accurately express it *without learning how to do so with his own hands?* How is he to train his own eye by the use of some one's else hands?

Formal rendering may be considered as the foundation of all rendering and its principles may be applied with the proper intelligent modifications to freer work. The danger to avoid in doing too much formal rendering is the acquisition of a habit of too great precision. Therefore one must keep loosened up by plenty of rapid sketching. Let no lazy man think he can succeed in this any more than he can in anything else. Formal rendering is not for the lazy man.

After due consideration I have determined to assume that the reader is a beginner and knows little or nothing about rendering but wants to find out. This will give the novice what he needs—and the more experienced may find useful and helpful suggestions.

ARCHITECTURAL
RENDERING IN WASH

Will all you who have helped me make this book, by loan of drawings, by advice and criticism, by reading proof, and above all by friendly encouragement, accept my warmest thanks?

H. VAN BUREN MAGONIGLE.

1921.

ARCHITECTURAL RENDERING IN WASH

I

THE PRELIMINARY STEPS

A successful rendering begins 'way back with the bare drawing board. The careful man will choose the best board he can find. He will test the edges to see if they be true, free from bulges and hollows which would throw the T-square up or down, for accuracy is essential to complete success; friezes, or the narrow whites of cornices or flights of steps must be the same width throughout. He will clean the board carefully, remove old edges of former mounts and old paste. Then he will sandpaper it with fine sandpaper and if there are any humps in the surface, hammer them down carefully. Bad hollows and old thumb-tack holes may be filled up with a mixture of very thin glue (or very thick glue-water) and whiting, sandpapered smooth after drying.

Now why on earth these precautions? Because lumps and hummocks under the paper to be mounted on this board cause dirt and graphite to collect on the paper over the lumps, and such collections are very difficult to erase. Also, with a singular perversity, they always come in the worst possible places on the drawing. Also, old paste when dampened again by the wet paper sticks to the underside of it and the only way to part

3

them is to whittle a chip out of the board and pare it off of the paper.

Paper. All this labor may be delegated by those maintaining trusty slaves, but the work of the most trustworthy may be inspected and reviewed to advantage. The next step, however, is for the operator himself. It concerns the selection and mounting of the paper. Of all the papers in the world the best for rendering is Whatman's cold-pressed. Hot-pressed Whatman is merely the same paper run through hot rollers which crush down the surface and make it very smooth. When wet up the grain rises again somewhat. But, while admirable for certain classes of line drawings, it is not, in my opinion, a good surface to render upon in wash. It won't stand sponging very well, the smooth surface is easily abraded by the rubber and dirt collects upon it like magic. Whatman's cold-pressed comes in various sized sheets, the largest, called "Antiquarian," being 31 x 52 inches. This size sheet is just right for weight which can be obtained in the smaller sizes when ordered "Extra Heavy." The smaller sheets are called "Double Elephant," 27 x 40 inches, and Imperial 22 x 30 inches. Thin, light-weight paper should be avoided even for very small drawings. It lacks quality of surface somehow, and will buckle and bulge when wet up with a wash because it has no body. For very large drawings it is sometimes necessary to use roll papers. Most of them are to be avoided. Whatman makes a good roll paper which lacks the quality of the hand-made sheet paper but has a fairly good surface. Eggshell paper was the best roll paper; it had texture, would stand hard usage and come up smiling to take a wash beautifully. Steinbach is not fit to use. It gets brittle with age and splits if stretched very tight—but its great defect is a deceptive air of receptiveness to a wash. It looks as though it would be great—but it is so non-absorbent that the washes won't dry and you get run-backs and fans. This is true of most roll papers—the surface is too hard. The grain of the paper greatly affects the quality and liveliness of the wash. The identical mixture laid in the identical manner on different kinds of paper looks entirely different when dry.

Joining Sheets. It is worth making a great many sacrifices to use Whatman's—changing the scale of the drawing if necessary and possible, to get it on a single large sheet. When the drawing has to be larger than a single Antiquarian sheet I would rather paste two or more together than use any roll paper now obtainable. This joining should be done by an expert, but when an expert is not at hand one may make shift for one's self. The two edges to be joined should have the rough deckle edge trimmed off square and then beveled down to a feather edge with fine emery paper, the edges retrimmed and then pasted together very carefully with Higgins's Drawing Board Paste, as it comes from the jar, spread on with a knife blade and the joint thumbtacked down at the extreme ends until dry, when any paste that has squeezed out of the joint must be carefully sponged off with a damp, not a wet, sponge. The best thing now is to paste it solid (or "float" it, as some say) on a mount made up of three or more thicknesses of cardboard glued or pasted together. To such a mount, which is in itself larger than most drawing boards, lighter and more wieldly, may be clamped a straight edge on which to work the T-square—and for a big drawing the straight edge may be shifted around for greater convenience. It is perhaps unnecessary to say that the joint (or joints) in the paper will be arranged to come where it will be least conspicuous in the drawing, that it will be parallel to the edge of the sheet, the mount and the horizontals or verticals of the drawing, and that if the joint is horizontal, the top half of the sheet will lap over the bottom half—the reason, of course, being that since most washes are run from the top of the drawing down, the wash slips over the edge of the joint. If it were the other way, the color would gather in a streak and perhaps cause a run-back. There will inevitably be a slight ridge along the lap and this will get very black and dirty unless great care is used as indicated later.

Cloth-backed Papers. Some prefer to work entirely on paper mounted solid. And in this connection there is a warning to sound: Be careful that the paste is not worked up into the paper. If it is, stop right there. The drawing will be a botch. Also, cloth-backed papers are dangerous to use because they are made by the yard by running them through pressure rollers which make a fine job of the pasting, but squeeze the paste right through. I prefer to mount the paper by the edges on a drawing board, because then I know there is no paste in the paper and because one is left freer in the matter of mounting the drawing afterward—for one may ink in a cutting line and run the washes out over it regardless, trim the drawing to the line, mount it solid on a white mount which will give, when the outer paper border is pasted on, a white band of any desired width next to the drawing—which is very valuable to have—and which white band may be modified in tone by drawing lines or washing-in bands upon it.

I advocate mounting *joined* sheets solid to work upon, because the tensions in a joined sheet are so queer that it is very hard to mount by the edges only on a board (if you can get a board big enough) and then, when the drawing is cut off, the shrinkages of the two or more pieces differ so owing to the disparity in the number of washes passed over the various parts, that it is harder to mount than before the drawing is made on it and to which original difficulty is added the fact that a valuable drawing is now on one side of it.

Selecting the Paper. Let us assume that we can use a single sheet of Whatman's of any size you like under 31 x 52″ but Extra Heavy. The first thing to do is to select the sheet carefully from among a goodly number. Every sheet of Whatman is dated in the marginal water mark. Hold it to the light. The older the paper the better dried out and seasoned it is. Some thoughtful persons lay down a few sheets a year as our forebears laid down wine to ripen and mellow. And although Whatman's is a singularly agreeable white and holds its color wonderfully (which, by the way, eggshell did not), it does take on a slightly creamier tone with age. Hold it to the light again and examine it carefully for defects. Sometimes in the process of manufacture, a drop of water falls on the soft pulp and makes a thin spot which resembles a little crater; sometimes the film of pulp is thinner in places; and nearly always there are specially thick places and little lumps and sometimes dark or black spots. These are defects inseparable from a hand-made paper. Frequently lumps which seem to be a part of the fabric may be picked off with a careful finger nail. When the thin spots are pretty bad or numerous, return the paper to the dealer. One can nearly always find a perfect or practically perfect sheet or avoid trouble by choosing one in which the defect will occur in a part of the drawing where it will do the least harm.

Mounting. Having selected a good sheet we mount it on

the board. The best way to mount a sheet of paper is always one's own way. Nevertheless the following has its advantages and has, besides, the cachet of Professor William R. Ware's recommendation; I caught it from a pupil of his when very young and am incurably addicted to it. Lay the paper on the board with the water mark right side up and turn up the edges carefully all around making a soft crease so that they will stand up and form a shallow pan (one-half or three-quarters of an inch wide; it is not necessary to trim off the deckle edges). At this point Professor Ware would have us turn the sheet over and wet it on the other side, the side next to the drawing board when mounted, the theory being not to sponge the working face more than can be helped. (But Whatman likes to be sponged and prospers under it if it isn't actually scrubbed while wet. Another part of the theory was that in this way the edges did not get wet and dilute the paste or soften up so that when you rubbed them down to make the paste stick they would tear. My experience is, first, that the water on the back leaks out under the edges when they are turned down again and causes just these troubles; second, that the wet surface clings to the board and makes it harder to stretch; and third, that the paper wets the board, sometimes causing the grain of the wood to rise and frequently discoloring the paper.) I therefore diverge at this point and wet the paper on the working face, but in the Ware manner, viz., with a clean sponge full of clean water make the British Union Jack—or those of anti-British predilections may run the sponge from corner to corner and on the two main axes of the sheet; the result will be the same. Do it slowly and pass the sponge over the wet bands several times. Then let the water soak in for a minute or two and sponge the whole sheet all over, Union Jack and all. The theory is that from corner to corner and from side to side there will be a strip of paper about twice as wet as the rest, which therefore dries out last and in its final shrinking helps to strain the sheet to the corners and outer edges. Anyway it seems to work perfectly. The sheet being wet all over, squeeze spongefuls of water on it so as to cover it with a thin film of water. The sheet will buckle and form puddles. Keep the puddles moving with the sponge and keep the outer turned-up edges dry. When the paper is thoroughly soaked and limp, sop up the surplus water with the squeezed-out sponge until no more actual puddles form. Have a towel handy and *keep your hands clean*. While the paper is soaking, if you forgot it before, get out the Higgins's Drawing Board Paste. Use it practically as it comes in the jar. Dampen your paste brush and rub it around in the jar.

Adjust the paper square with the edges of the board, and pin the center of one long edge to the board with two thumb-tacks a couple of inches apart. Put paste along the opposite turned-up edge for eight inches or a foot. Take hold of it, lift the paper slightly and pull gently but strongly, put the gummed edge down on the board, and hold it firmly with one hand while you put in a couple of thumbtacks to hold it. Seize a piece of clean paper, put it over the gummed edge and with some smooth object like a knife handle, rub gently at first and then more strongly. As soon as the paper adheres enough, take out the thumbtacks on this side and rub down where they were. Turn the board around, take out the two thumbtacks from that edge, pull gently but strongly again, and paste it just as you did the other, including use of thumbtacks. Do the same at the center of the two ends. Work quickly. Watch the paper. Water will, if you have wet it properly, gather in the hollows. Sop it up with the sponge. Go back to the sides and paste down enough of each edge at each side of the center to leave four to six inches unpasted at the corners. Do the same on the ends, always pulling the paper gently but strongly before laying the edge down and rubbing it till it adheres.

Some false prophets will tell you the paper should merely be laid down and never pulled and that the water shrinkage is enough. Don't listen to them. They don't know what they are talking about. Try it some time. Make a careful drawing on a big sheet, float the first big wash and give me the news. It will buckle and form puddles. Even a damp day will make it buckle.

After this disgression we will paste down the corners, putting the paste on both corner edges and pulling as the appearance of the paper indicates, straight to the corner or more on one or the other side as required to take out fullness.

If properly done, the sheet should now be fairly flat all over without puckers anywhere along the edges, and should show no dirty finger prints nor be bedaubed with paste. If paste has gotten on sponge it off gently with a damp, not wet, sponge. The sheet may still be wet enough for faint puddles to collect. If not removed they will dry out leaving yellowish or shiny rings. Sop them up with a sponge, not blotting paper as the thoughtless operator does. Blotting paper is apt to deposit a fuzz on the paper and the pressure required often makes creases in the damp and buckled paper of which just enough remain to spoil a sky or background wash later. Either let it dry naturally (*lying down flat* so that the moisture won't run to one side), or set an electric fan going at low speed, far enough away so that the cone of moving air will play over the whole surface. Don't point the fan directly down at it; let it blow over it. Inspect it every once in a while till it is dry. Some parts of the paper may have quite dried up before the rest. Dampen them till they are like the rest of the sheet. If puckers show near the edge dampen them thoroughly and if not too bad they will shrink out.

Again it may be asked, Why such care? And why not let a mere worm like the office boy do it? Sometimes he must but whenever there is time, do it yourself. I count my own time worth something—but when I have an important drawing to make, I mount the paper myself. Then I know what I have. I know it is equally stretched, I know it is well pulled, I know the paste is not two or three inches wide on the edges or drops of it here and there under the paper, I know the damp paper has not been scarified by careless handling. To be sure, if something goes wrong there is no one else to blame and that I confess is a drawback. No one detests drudgery more than the writer but this is craftsmanship and part of the job of making a perfect rendered drawing.

Cleanliness. While the paper is drying is a good time to clean the T-square and triangles and scale. If of wood, use gasoline to avoid warping, and wipe off thoroughly to remove any possible greasy residue. Celluloid triangles may be washed in soap and water. Don't overlook the edges. Absolute cleanliness from start to finish is essential to success. T-squares and triangles covered with months' or years' deposit of graphite and grease no real draughtsman will tolerate. The hands should be washed frequently enough to keep them really clean. Once grease gets in the paper, you may bid success good-by; lines will crumble and crawl when you ink in and washes won't take.

Transferring Studies to Final Paper. The final paper on which you are making the rendering is no place to study the design. Accurate and careful studies should be made before you start the rendered drawing, so that you have only to copy or at the most make the last delicate adjustments of whites and grays —and these you make on tick-strips. Some people use a scale and some use dividers. I don't like a drawing pricked full of holes, so I use both scale and tick-strip. For the accurate transfer of vertical and horizontal subdivisions, take a strip of paper (ticker tape is good or a strip of tracing paper folded with a sharp true edge) long enough to go entirely across the drawing whether lengthwise or sidewise. Thumbtack it at the ends over the study and, using T-square or triangle as the case may be, with a hard sharp pencil draw the lines you want to transfer on the edge of the tick-strip. If they are to be changed slightly on the final drawing, here is the place to do it. Mark the lines or groups of lines so as to identify them, not forgetting to put on the position of the working line. Then pin this strip over your final paper top-and-bottom or side-and-side, with the working line coinciding with that of which you have already established the position on the final paper, and reproduce on your final paper the lines on the tick-strip.

Whites in Pitches of Platforms, Foregrounds, etc. When landings occur in flights of steps, it is advisable to express the fact that there is a break in their continuity by introducing a space between the bottom of the riser at the far side of the landing and the top of the riser at the near side, which will be wider in the drawing than the actual pitch would be in execution. This

PLATE I   RENDERED BY OTTO R. EGGERS

Messrs. York & Sawyer's Competition Elevation of the Federal Reserve Bank

A beautiful example of Mr. Eggers' rendering and one he considers representative.   The line drawing was made by R. A. Tissington, who prepared it for rendering by shade-lining it very carefully.

space to express and indicate the landings is, when rendered, made much lighter than the steps themselves. A similar convention is observed in the pitch of the sidewalks or of roadbeds running parallel with the face of the building or of foregrounds or similar spaces. These must be carefully studied in advance and decided upon before the final drawing is penciled in. It is necessary to make quite a number of small adjustments in order to effect the desired result without misrepresenting the facts. In a flight of steps, for example, it may be managed by omitting one or two of the risers in elevation, adding their height to the normal or true amount of the pitch of the landing, thus securing a wider white than any in the whole flight of steps without altering the total height. The width of the treads which belong to these two omitted risers will have to be redistributed among the other spaces or thrown into the width of the landings. It is well also to make the top fillets of cornices and the like much wider than they would be in execution in order to give a brilliant light along the top of the cornice.

Studies at Larger Scale. Of course, I have here assumed that the final drawing, an elevation, is being made at the same scale as the study. But often the study is at a larger scale. My own practice is always to make a study of a portion at a larger scale. If the final drawing is sixteen feet to the inch, I usually make an eighth scale study and often certain parts at quarter scale. There is a certain amount of translation and simplification to do in reducing it, certain eliminations of members and detail, but nothing makes a small scale drawing look so real or gives it so much scale as to reduce it from a larger scale study. The experienced man will simply reduce the principal elements, getting the accurate relations of greys to whites—as in the main divisions of architrave, frieze and cornice and their subdivisions—in short get the *character*. The principal individual members will then fall into place. But this work should be done on a separate piece of paper and then ticked off on a tick-strip as indicated above. It is just as easy to get too many as too few lines in a drawing. When it is rendered a drawing simplifies materially and if there is too little drawing it looks thin and meager. But too many lines in too small a space will make it look clogged and lifeless especially in places where there should be a brilliant reflected light as in the bed moldings of a cornice. Experience is the only teacher here, in the absence of competent personal counsel.

Preserving the Surface of the Paper. The surface of the paper must be preserved in perfect condition. Dirt and grease and the friction of T-square and triangle and scale and elbows and instruments will wear off the slight calendering the paper has received and make it so pulpy that both lines and washes will spread as though on blotting paper. For this reason the paper must be protected in any of several ways, such as by pinning strips of tracing paper across the parts you are not working upon and shifting them as required, or cutting openings with flaps in a shield of detail paper big enough to cover the whole board. Any way that is most convenient and that you like best provided it keeps the drawing clean. Erasures should be just as few as possible, and be lightly and carefully made and the rubber dust brushed off with a soft desk brush or flapped off with a fresh handkerchief—I like the handkerchief best.

Penciling In. This is not a manual of line draughtsmanship and it is assumed that the man who is about to render knows how to draw. And yet I have seen men highly rated as draughts-men who had not the faintest realization of the importance of careful cleanly methods in the preparation of a drawing that is to receive washes. Pencils are made of graphite and graphite is used to lubricate automobile chains. If you get too much graphite on your drawing you will so lubricate it that when you come to ink in the ink won't take and you'll wonder per-haps why you can't get a good clean line with vigor and char-acter and delicacy in it. That is one reason why. Use a 3H, 4H or 5H pencil depending upon the weather. On damp days the paper absorbs the moisture in the air and the softer grade is hard enough; on hot dry days a 3H often seems soft and crumbly. Draw with a light hand. Make as faint a drawing as you can read clearly enough to ink in accurately. Perfect accuracy, to assure the uniform width of spacings, windows, flutes of columns and the like, is assumed. And get into the habit, until it be-comes unconscious and instinctive, of lifting your T-square and triangle from line to line; you will thus avoid wearing down and blurring a light drawing and spreading graphite all over the paper. A rubbing strip of detail paper doubled over and pinned down top and bottom at both ends of the T-square helps to keep it from rubbing the paper.

Keep your drawing *all* covered up when you are not work-ing on it. If you don't, dirt will settle upon it.

It is a good plan to lift your protecting shield or strips from time to time and brush off underneath. Even with the utmost care the opening is soon seen to be defined on the white paper as a light grey patch.

Rubbing On. The practise of "rubbing on" ("frothing" [1]

[1] Apparently a corruption of the French *frotter*, to rub.

so-called) or transferring a pencil study made on tracing paper is not worthy of consideration in the kind of drawing we are here discussing. It does very well for the average drawing made *en charrette*.[1] It also does well enough for many drawings made in the run of office work. By this method, penciling-in on final paper is almost entirely eliminated. The final study is made on tracing paper (with everything reversed if the design is not symmetrical), turned over face down on the final paper, and rubbed on the back with the edge of a key top, or of a smooth coin or something of the sort until the pencil rubs off; the human thumb-nail is probably the best instrument. Dampening the paper slightly will assist the process of transfer and holds the line—but of course buckles and expands the study somewhat. A piece of tracing cloth should be interposed between the rubbing instrument and the study. The rubbing damages the surface of the paper and frequently causes ridges or hollows which will never come out.

Transfer Paper. Another way is to slip a sheet or a number of sheets of carbon paper under the study and with a very hard sharp pencil go over every line of the latter. This gets a lot of carbon on the paper. The French have a very attractive reddish-brown transfer paper of about the color of *sanguine* which is far better than black for this sort of thing. A rapid, crisp transfer made in this way with this paper, a few light

---

[1] For the benefit of the uninitiated I will explain this term so often heard and so wonderfully mispronounced. The drawings made in the various *ateliers* or studios related to the Ecole des Beaux Arts are taken to the latter in a little hand-cart or *charrette* which waits down in the courtyard while the drawings are being finished. Drawings sometimes actually receive their last touches while on the cart on its way through the streets. Hence the expression "*en charrette*" as applied to something done in a tearing hurry.

shadows, a little *"piquage,"* [1] a suggestive sketchy background and you have a very attractive sketch—but not a perfect rendered drawing.

Lightening Up. The drawing completed in pencil, it may be lightened and made fainter if necessary by dabbing it softly with a soft rubber or the so-called "art" gum and carefully and lightly dusted off to leave no particles to be taken up by the ruling- or freehand-pen and spoil a line.

Toning the Ink. The next step is to prepare the ink. Higgins's Waterproof Ink is perfectly satisfactory. It has a very good tone in itself, but I prefer to tone it to suit conditions. We will assume for the purpose of exposition that the drawing is an elevation, at sixteenth scale, of a light stone building with a central motif with some columns in antis projecting strongly from the general mass, with two wings at each side pierced with windows, and that some distance back of the face of these wings another portion of the building, say an auditorium wall, rises higher than the central motif. (See Diagram B, facing p. 34.) At every step we take in the drawing we are making it ready to receive the washes which will bring out the values of the planes, model the building, give it three dimensions. You will work uphill and under a handicap and your drawing will not be so fine if you do not give the planes their values while it is still in pure line. You will, of course, dilute the ink from the pure black of the bottle, dilute it 'way down. For the plane furthest back the ink should be lighter and colder; the planes in advance of this should be successively darker and warmer. If the re-

---

[1] This is a French expression derived from the verb *piquer* (pronounced Pee-kay). I know no single word in English which expresses just what this means; approximately, to pick out accents. The process of piquage (pronounced Pee-kazh) will be found described on pp. 76-78-89.

moter planes are far enough back to warrant it, as at the back
of a deep court formed by a U-shaped building, the Higgins's
Ink may be cooled by the addition of a little blue—Cobalt or
Ultramarine—never Prussian or any of the green blues. There
is nothing so unpleasant as a greenish black line or wash. The
ink for the first plane may be warmed by the addition of Burnt
Sienna and a touch of Carmine. Burnt Sienna, while warm in
itself, gives the ink, when the two happen to be in certain proportions, a slightly greenish cast which the Carmine corrects.
Test out the color of the toned ink by drawing lines of various
widths on the margin of the sheet (or another piece of Whatman) *drawing the lines at the speed you will use when you
begin to ink in.*

The Line and Its Quality. Determine the width of the
line you intend to use. There is a good deal of buncombe current about the use of a thick line. Men coming back from Paris,
accustomed to seeing merely effective drawings, which wouldn't
bear inspection, made under charrette conditions, went about
prating wisely of strong lines in âtelier French. Anything less
than a sixteenth of an inch wide these little masters called "wiry."
If they had had the wit to examine the best drawings in the
world—the *envois* made by the *Grand Prix* men and of which
reproductions are now available to us in D'Espouy, and those
by Viollet-le-Duc in the *Musée du Trocadero,* they would have
seen "wiry" lines by the thousand. It doesn't matter how thin
a line is so long as it has quality and beauty. Some men never
learn to draw a line that has either. It is something in the angle
at which the pen is held, something in the touch, the amount of
pressure exerted, the slight crisp lift at the end of the line to
avoid a dark dot. Some men bite a line hard into the paper.

Even a thick line is wiry under that treatment. A firm even pressure is required which carries the ink down into all the little hollows of the surface; which does not skip along the high spots and give the line an inexpressibly mean and crumbly appearance. While you are not setting out to make a line drawing, you want to make a beautiful drawing—and that means one of which all the elements are beautiful. The line, in quality and value, is one of the elements. In a wash drawing the light and shade are what should count. In a quick and hasty rendering such as one must make sometimes, when one has to cast a few shadows and pass a tone or two in summary fashion, the line has to count and count strongly, to give the drawing vigor, the shadows on such a drawing always being made pretty light by the knowing man. But in the serious drawing such as we are discussing, when we have plenty of time, the line should not be obvious. It should be just firm enough to keep the drawing from being woolly.

Planes versus Lines. Look carefully at a real building. The cornice is not composed of lines but of a series of bands of light and shade and shadow. These may have sharp edges—but neither Nature nor the builder has ruled a dark line along every edge. One surface lighted in a certain way meets another surface lighted in a different way and there is no line properly so called—certainly not a line of another value—at the junction. I have tried thick very pale lines and thin pale lines and thick and thin dark ones and I'm for a thin pale line. I think it is easier to follow with a wash. When the line is thick and light your wash runs over on to the line in places and looks slovenly. The wash in this case should, of course, "consume the line," that is, be carried to the far side of it, but it is very difficult to do, just as hard as to follow the near edge. As for value, I like it just dark enough to be both firm and delicate after it is sponged down ready for rendering.

Fashions in drawings change with the years, but the drawings reproduced in D'Espouy have stood the test of the years with their changing fashions—and the line in the best of them is delicate and does not count as line.

The Ruling Pen. But the width of the line is a matter of taste and of temperament and of the scale of the drawing. I merely express my belief that coarse lines in small-scale elevations and sections kill the scale of the design. On the other hand, in small scale plans, wide soft lines in certain places and used in certain ways are wholly desirable. This matter will be found treated of under the rendering of plans. The tool itself has something to do with the line. It must be sharp but not too sharp. It must have a thick stiff back- or under-nib so that the pressure against the T-square won't open and close the pen as the pressure varies from end to end of the line. The Altṣneder (an American-made) ruling pen is made like this. If too sharp the pen will actually cut the paper.

Free-hand Pens. The best pens for the freehand portions of the drawing are, I think, Gillott's, especially the crow-quill pens which come, a dozen on a card, with a holder. They are adapted to the most delicate work or that of a coarser nature. A freehand pen of rather soft steel soon dulls, or sometimes is not even when new quite sharp enough to make a line fine enough for the occasion. It may be very simply sharpened by whetting the *sides* of the nibs back and forth a couple of times on the bare edge of the drawing board. And by whetting it the other way, it may be coarsened materially—the width of the point of each nib is reduced in the one case and widened in the latter. It is well to pass the point of any freehand pen once or twice through the flame of a match not merely to remove the film of oil there is on every new pen but also to take out the temper a bit and give it less excuse to sputter. In rendering plans it is frequently advisable to use a very much coarser nib, even as coarse as a ball-pointed pen.

Shade-Line Drawings. It is a very beautiful device to make a shade-line drawing for rendering; not carried to the limit as though it were to be left in line, but with certain lines strengthened so as to assist the modeling, particularly lines representing projections too slight to make it advisable to cast and render their shadows, such as the shadow side of rustication or small moldings here or there. A shade-line along the corona of a cornice helps to bring it forward. But all this is very easy to exaggerate and must be done with the utmost taste and judgment.

Joint Lines. Joint lines should be thinner and paler than the main architectural lines and be in relative value to the planes in which they occur, stronger for the nearer planes, lighter for those farther off. In a very quick rendering the joints may be made a good deal of and help to "furnish" the drawing. But in a good drawing the joints should have no more value than they have in Nature. Chifflot is as responsible as any one, I think, for the fashion of making the joints count for almost as much as the architecture—just as he made fashionable for a while very narrow stone courses which gave immense apparent scale to the design. But no one should care to make his building look as though it were built of that lovely invention, rock-faced brick. If it is a stone building, it should look stony of course. Study

Nature and be guided. If the building is brick we will discuss the joints when we come to talk about actual rendering.

Silhouettes. After the drawing is all inked in it is usually the fashion to silhouette the various parts of the building such as projecting pavilions, the general outline and so on, with a darker line. This is a practise of which I approve in line drawings and one I have followed for years in rendered drawings also—but I have come to believe it a mistake in a really serious rendered drawing. It is a heresy that has crept in on the infernal charrette—when will we ever be rid of its malign influence? In the hasty rendering in the schools (and they are always hasty for some or another bad reason) the silhouette is indispensable to help bring out the values of planes there is no time or skill to express properly. I believe it makes a more beautiful, a more real, a more convincing, drawing to let the roof meet the sky as in Nature, plane be relieved against plane as in Nature, by the accurate value of the tones. Nature sometimes softens an edge but no one ever caught her drawing silhouettes around things.

Cleaning Off. The inking in completed, the pencil lines must be rubbed out where they show and the drawing "dry-cleaned" before sponging off. The cleaning off should be done just as carefully as any other part of the process. "Art gum" is an excellent thing to clean with, used very lightly; a fresh Ruby rubber will take off the pencil lines which do not yield to it— a green rubber is a bit too hard. Go over every inch of surface, and examine the drawing in different lights to make sure it is clean. Then you are ready to sponge off unless you have decided to do what is very rarely done and ink in the outlines of the cast shadows; we will come to that matter presently.

PLATE 2   BY THE AUTHOR

Formal rendering is not usually associated with Gothic subjects and this drawing of an angle of
the Ducal Palace in Venice is therefore given as an example.   All the shadows, except the window
shadows which are toned with blue, were toned with vermilion, and after a lapse of twenty-five
years are as fresh and warm as at first.

Sponging Off. Tilt the board at an angle of ten or fifteen degrees. Take a good-sized bowl, or a large shallow casserole with a handle (which is the best thing I know of to hold the water for mounting, for sponging off, for use in rendering, and for washing the brush in), fill it with water and with a soft sponge—a face sponge—just as full as it will hold, run it along the top of the drawing and then, keeping the sponge always full, float the water down over the drawing very gently. Some lines and places where there is a good deal of detail will run slightly. Unless the paper is positively flooded with a film of water of an appreciable depth over it, such lines and places will merely smear and the ink get into the paper where it is almost impossible to get it out. Parts of the drawing where a great many lines make a dark patch may be materially reduced in value by carefully sponging them down—and of course any line or group of lines. Wet the paper all over, right out to the edge. When you are sure no more superfluous ink will float off the lines, squeeze out your sponge and begin to sop up the water gently. The board should not have been tilted so that the water would run off at the bottom in streams. Don't rub the drawing with the sponge. Just sop and squeeze until it is all off and then watch it to remove the puddles which will form in the same way as in mounting the paper. Then lay it flat, under a slow fan if you like, till dry.

The object in sponging off is to remove any possible grease, to remove superfluous ink which would otherwise run when you pass a wash over it, and to give the paper an additional shrinking so that it will be sure to lie flat and not form hollows for puddles to gather in when the big washes go on.

Alum. It is an excellent thing to dissolve about a table-

admirable. It holds water enough and is fine enough to get into the smallest corners if properly selected. For large washes there is nothing better than the camel's hair brushes which the French make in quills into which a wooden handle is thrust. The larger brushes of the same sort are bound to the handle with wire. They hold an enormous quantity of wash and come to a wonderful point. They haven't enough spring for general use in rendering, and, carrying as much moisture as they do, it is very hard to control the gradation of a small wash with them. We will refer to this point later.

Selecting a Brush. It pays to spend some time and trouble in the selection of a brush, for brushes of the same size vary enormously in quality and characteristics. Some are generous and let the water flow out of them freely. Others suck up a lot but won't give it up easily. Others again won't hold much and let it come out in blobs. Some will come to a fine point, and others won't point up at all. And these characteristics effect other combinations for the confusion of man. To select a brush, pick it out of a dozen or a hundred. Put it in a tumbler of water and wabble it around to get the air out of it and thoroughly soak the hairs. Take it out and hold it with the point of the brush upright. The point should be perfect and the brush smooth and symmetrical. Go through a lot of them in the same way, laying aside those that won't point up well. Then proceed to eliminate from the best ones until you find a perfect one which will carry plenty of water, give it up easily and keep a sharp and symmetrical point under all conditions. Try it also on paper, laying a wash of water, and see how it acts, and also how it acts when you wipe it off on the edge of the glass. Nothing but a perfect brush is worth having.

Some of the Chinese bristle brushes are excellent for skies and big washes if you can get a good one. They come with a gluey dressing in them which has to be washed out. If neither French nor Chinese are available, then a big Red Sable brush is, of course, fine, provided it stands the tests indicated above. But the really large ones are quite expensive.

Care of the Brush. Take the best of care of your brushes. When not in use keep them in a box with camphor or moth balls in it. Don't let them kick around in a drawer or stand around where moths can get at them. When you are using a brush, get into the habit until it becomes mechanical of washing it out every time you pick it up to use or lay it down when you stop for a moment. Otherwise India Ink will soon dry among the hairs and some day when you are laying a delicate tone dried particles will float out. And never under any circumstances leave it standing on its hairs in a glass of water. A really good brush is hard to make, hard to find, and such treatment deforms it.

India Ink. Then as to ink, called India Ink because, one may suppose, it is made chiefly in China and Japan. Chinese ink is believed to be the best. It varies greatly in quality and quite a bit in color. The softer, poorer grade sticks are usually warmer in color than the more expensive. If you can find a hard, high grade stick of a warm tone, hide it. It is worth keeping for yourself. The trouble with buying ink is that you can't try it out before purchase, for it is beautifully gilded all over and there is no way to know. But get as expensive a stick as you feel you can afford. Better a small good one than a large fat cheap one. And as to the tone, it doesn't much matter after all because you will tone it anyway; the warmer the original tone, however, the less water color pigment we need to warm it up and that is an advantage in transparency.

Rubbing up the Ink. To prepare the ink for use, take a shallow saucer made of slate, which is obtainable at any dealer in architects' supplies, put a tablespoonful of clean water in it and rub the ink around until the water seems black. Dip a brush in it and try it on a piece of white paper. It should dry out a very dark grey, practically black, to be right. Pour this off into a tumbler and cover it over. Grind four or five table-spoonfuls, which should be enough to last through a large draw-ing. Take another perfectly clean and freshly rinsed tumbler and spread over the mouth a piece of muslin—a small piece of tracing cloth thoroughly washed out is excellent—depress the muslin a bit to form a shallow cup and wet the center of it to facilitate capillary action. Then pour in the ground ink slowly and let it drip through. When it is all through gather up the edges of the rag and wash the rag out thoroughly in running water. Also the first tumbler. Put the rag over the empty tum-bler as you did before and strain the strained ink again. Repeat four, five or six or more times as may be necessary until, as you tip the tumbler, there are no particles visible in the thin film of fluid on the side of the glass. Then it is fit to use.

Don't forget to wipe off the stick carefully after grinding and dry it with a rag as thoroughly as possible, else your costly stick will crack into small bits.

Keeping Ink. India Ink evaporates very quickly. To keep it from doing so, put two or three pieces of blotting paper sop-ping wet over the top of the glass and put a weight upon it, such as a color saucer. Re-wet the blotters the last thing at night and in the morning and through the day if necessary—as it will be in warm weather. *Always keep it covered up,* and you will have a perfect, clean, limpid fluid to work with.

Blotters and Their Uses. Provide yourself with half a dozen large white blotters and a package of small white ones. It is much more convenient when running a large wash to have your water bowl and *godets* (pronounced "goday" and meaning a color saucer) nearer to it than they would be if off your board on the table. A couple of these large blotters may be placed upon the drawing, and the water bowl and godets upon them, and danger of splashes and spots will be thus avoided. The small blotters are useful in several ways. First and foremost to keep always under one's hand while working so that grease from the skin does not get into the paper, to help in mending and patching bad places in the wash, and to take up surplus wash from the brush; by this I mean that when a brush is recharged with wash even after it has been wiped on the edge of the godet or vessel containing it, you may find, when you come to apply it to the paper that there is just a little too much fluid in it; this is specially to be observed in grading a wash; exactly the right amount of water is essential, because if there is too much, the new part of the wash will run back into the old part, creating a fan or run-back. By touching the brush to the blotter you can satisfactorily control the wetness. Always be sure that the blotter is absolutely clean on the side which touches the drawing.

Cleanliness Again. Be sure to dust off your table and board and all your surroundings frequently, and *keep them clean.* Wet brushes, laid down on dirty, dusty surfaces, pick up the dirt and transfer it to the drawing.

Pigments as Toning Agents. In a later chapter will be found a discussion of the properties of pigments. Of all the colors examined there are only a few we need as toning agents for our ink washes in formal rendering. These are, in my practise,

Carmine	Raw Sienna	Cobalt Blue
Burnt Sienna		French Blue

and very occasionally Viridian and Chinese White.

It is to be assumed that before a man begins a serious piece of rendering he will have tried out his colors in various ways and learned something of what they will do. But this sort of practise is, of course, very like mashie and putting practise at golf. It takes the stern fiber of a Walter Travis to go out and just practise for hours and hours. The average man prefers to play a game and learn as he goes. And most men learn to render, not by practising laying washes but by making bad drawing after drawing until somehow or other they learn to make a good one.

II

RENDERING

Values. The "value" of a tone has been defined by Denman Ross as the *quantity* of light in it and the "color" of a tone as the *quality* of light in it. Formal, academic rendering in monotone is a study in values. Values and nothing else. The relative value of plane to plane, with no adventitious aids. The architecture to be rendered by such a method has to be pretty good, pretty carefully studied. Accurately and honestly cast shadows reveal defects and bring out beauties impartially. The principal use to which this type of rendering should be applied is of course the serious study of a piece of architecture for one's own behoof—not merely for the swell presentation of competition drawings or for the amazement of a client. (The kind of lies the drawings are often made to tell in the latter instances would be precisely like cheating at solitaire in the first.) Therefore the whole process of rendering, from white paper to the finish, is the building up of values.

Pure Monotone. I shall treat of rendering an elevation at sixteenth scale in pure India Ink, merely toned, first, before dealing with the modification of this method in which a considerable amount of color is used.

Monotone and Monochrome. Curiously, there is considerable confusion of mind in many quarters, a confusion not by any means confined to those of tender years, as to the difference between monotone and monochrome. Mono-chrome means *one* *color.* Mono-tone means *one tone.* If we substitute "pigment" for "color" it will make things clearer. If you render a drawing entirely in Burnt Sienna you make both a monotone and a monochrome. If you use a mixture of Burnt Sienna and French Blue you make a mono*tone* drawing but not a mono*chrome* because you have used more than one color or pigment to produce a certain tone. A drawing in pure India Ink as it comes from the stick is in monochrome and in monotone—one tone, one pigment. If you add pigment to the ink to change its tone you are no longer working in monochrome but in monotone.

India Ink. When we last heard of the India Ink we had ground, it was all strained and covered up ready to use.

It must be remembered that India Ink dries out many shades lighter than it appears to be when wet. It takes much practise to train the judgment to a point where one can strike exactly the right value at once. Of course, when washes are built up by running one pale wash over another, this is discounted to a certain extent, but there are some parts of the process in which this knowledge of exactly how dark to make a wash is absolutely essential. This applies particularly to the last process a drawing undergoes which is "Piquage."

A beginner is easily deceived also by the fact that a wash run over another so freshens up the latter that it seems either too dark or dark enough. Pure water will have a similar effect.

The Mother Wash. We take a godet of which we have a nest of half a dozen ready, and fill it partly full of clean water. With a perfectly clean brush we take out a partial brushful of the ink, put it in the water and mix it up thoroughly. Then we try it on a piece of Whatman paper, grade it out to very pale and let it dry. When dry we decide whether it needs warming and how much—or for those who like cold drawings, how much it needs cooling. If it is to be warmed, put a little Burnt Sienna and a touch of Carmine in the glass of India Ink and mix thoroughly. The darker you have ground the ink the more pigment it will take to modify the color. Until you have enough experience to know just about how much to put in first whack, it is better to build up gradually to the tone you want or you may spoil an hour's worth of ground ink. When it is to your liking as shown by the last little test wash you have laid, it is ready to use. If the ink is to be cooled, merely add either Cobalt or French Blue until it suits you; these are both heavy colors and very little is required to cool ink not so very warm at the best.

This glassful of toned ink is the "Mother Wash" for use throughout the drawing and will keep the drawing in tone.

Planning Out and Division of Washes. The beginner will waste a lot of color and ink at first and until he learns by experience how much wash to mix up for the different parts of the drawing. And it will be perhaps a commonplace of his early experience to find himself three-quarters through a big wash and his godet empty. If he is canny though, he will see his finish when he is half way through, take measures accordingly and begin to add water to his wash. If he stops in a panic and begins madly to mix up some more tone his finish merely comes right away. A man has to keep his head all the time and keep it at work thinking. Experience will soon tell how much wash to mix—when in doubt mix too much. Experience will teach how to plan ahead when you have a lot of separate tones of the same value or color to be graded in just the same way—such as window washes or the wall behind a colonnade. For such, mix up enough for the lot and take out into a separate godet what you need for the first one, add water to it to grade it out until you are through with that one, then throw out what is left, dry out the godet, and repeat the process.

Sometimes a wash for one reason or another has to be divided up into two or three parts and set aside until each is used in turn, each with exactly the same amount of color in it. ·When using heavy colors especially it may be difficult to hit the absolute shade a second time. A good way therefore is to stir up the wash thoroughly and then divide it by brushfuls, so many to each of the godets which are to hold the subdivided wash. Then as you grade, put in one brushful of clear water the first time you recharge your brush, two the next time and so on. You may then be pretty sure that your gradation is as nearly uniform as possible. Don't be afraid of this word, uniform, nor what is represents. Human tendency is all away from uniformity and so far as my observation goes in the use of water color by the young, the tendency is all toward sloppiness—which is not to be confused with freedom.

Beginning to Render. The wash is all ready to use and you think you are about to begin to render. Not at all! You are ready to begin to do some real thinking. 'And as an aid to thought it is an excellent idea to make preliminary studies of your rendering in carbon pencil, pretty carefully done, as a guide during the steps which follow.

We have assumed that the building is a simple one "of light stone with a central motif with some columns in antis, projecting strongly from the general mass, the two wings each side pierced with windows, and that some distance back of the face of these wings another portion of the building, say an auditorium

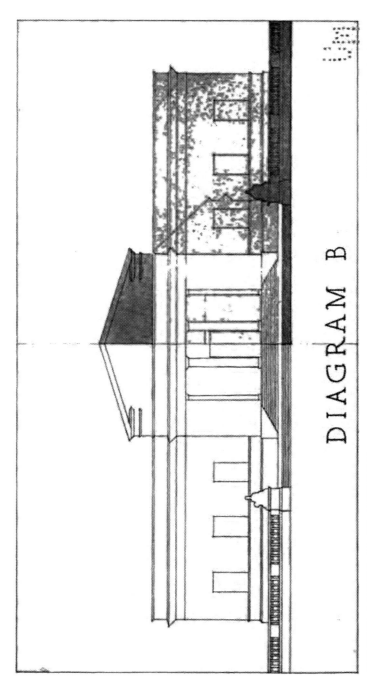

DIAGRAM B

BUILDING ASSUMED TO BE RENDERED

DRAWN BY OLIVER REAGAN

"A light stone building at 16th scale, with a central motif with some columns *in antis* projecting strongly from the general mass, with two wings at each side pierced with windows, and some distance back of the face of these wings another portion of the building, say an auditorium wall, rises higher than the central motif. Outside the building and well out in front, let us assume steps in the middle leading up to a terrace and at each side of them a balustrade with pedestals surmounted with sculpture."

wall, rises, higher than the central motif." (See Diagram B, facing page 34.)

We have therefore, in the building itself, three planes—that of the central motif, next furthest back the plane of the wings and the mass of the auditorium beyond these. Outside the building and well out in front, let us assume steps in the middle leading up to a terrace and at each side of them a balustrade with pedestals surmounted with sculpture.

Sky Tones. Behind the building we may assume a silhouette of the distant buildings of a city or merely some trees which show at each side, low down, 'way back. Beyond and *over* all of these planes is the sky—the sky from which the light comes, which is full of air, which is not a flat vertical backdrop as in stage scenery, which *arches over* all objects on earth, and which is usually represented in modern architectural renderings as nearly like midnight as possible, either built up wash after wash with a brush or blown on by air brush or atomizer and producing the effect of an opaque, black, flat curtain hung up behind a sheet of cardboard on which a drawing of a building is made. The mere fact that draughtsmen are in the habit of saying "background" when they mean "sky" indicates the common misconception. The labor of building up shadows and the local color of planes to a value which will hold with one of these coal scuttle skies is colossal. And men are driven to this kind of forced, airless, artificial, black type of rendering in self-defense—for it kills anything in its vicinity and makes a drawing in a reasonably light key look pale and sickly. And that is a bad thing to have happen to one's presentation in a competition or an exhibition. It is a convention in academic rendering to assume that a building is brilliantly illuminated by the sun, from the left, the light falling at an angle of 45° with the plane of the building. You will be entirely within your artistic right if you assume that although the sun is shining brightly over your left shoulder and casting shadows on your building, a typhoon or tornado is coming up behind it and that the sky in that quarter is black as night or lurid with impending storm. It is for you to decide whether you want a sky in your rendering with air in it, overarching the distance, middle distance and foreground and lighting your building, or a pot-black flat curtain hung up behind it. For the moment we will choose the sky.

All water color work is built up from light to dark. That is, the lightest tones are put on first, the darkest last. The surest way to begin any water color rendering, whether in ink or full color, is to put on a sky first, then the most distant objects (which are always colder and lighter than the nearer planes) and then the other planes as we come forward. This is a general principal subject to modifications which will be discussed further on. In this way you get, first the value of the sky which is to light the picture, than the value of the next most distant plane or object in relation to the sky, then the next plane—for which you have now two measures of value, the sky and the extreme distance, —and so on, the measures for comparison of value constantly increasing in number.

Now look out of the window at some building which has the sun upon it, some very light building. Study its value in relation to the sky. Under normal weather conditions, however light the building may be, the lower part of the sky toward the horizon, against which the building is seen, is lighter. If this is so then the sky will be the lightest part of the drawing-to-be.

Laying the Sky. Let us put on this sky, under which all the objects we subsequently render are to be seen. There are several ways of doing this. We may spray it on with an airbrush or atomizer or we may do it with a brush. Of the blown sky later; we are working just now with a brush. We may grade from dark to light or light to dark. In Nature a cloudless sky is lighter toward the horizon; the wash which represents it will be darkest at the top of the drawing and to get it we may either start at the top with dark ink and add water as we go down to grade it out to light, or we may start at the bottom with pale ink and add ink in as we go toward the top of the sky. The latter method is by all odds the best and safest.

We therefore turn the board around, block up the far edge so as to make the board tilt a little, say ten or fifteen degrees, take out a half teaspoonful or so of the Mother Wash and put it in one china saucer or godet and fill another godet about two-thirds full of clean water.

It is a very good idea to dampen the drawing by passing a very wet sponge over it very lightly immediately before beginning to lay the first wash and letting it dry till it is just faintly perceptibly damp to the backs of the fingers.

Take the brush you intend to lay the sky with, which should be one that will hold a lot of wash, and first wetting it thoroughly in your big bowl of water and then squeezing out all you can on the edge of the bowl (or slatting it on the floor, which is the best and quickest and most untidy way), put a very little of the ink from the godet into the one with the clean water—just enough to stain it a bit, barely cloud it. (The reason for taking some ink out and putting it in a godet is that the latter being shallow you can take ink up in your brush easily and see what you are doing and how much you are taking; and, there being always some lighter color in your brush in the course of the work we are now about to describe, it would run out into the Mother Wash every time you put your brush back into it and make it undergo a constant process of dilution so that when you want some really dark ink later on you haven't it and have to grind some more and tone it.) Work your brush around in it until what water was in it is all mingled with that in the godet and you are sure there is not a little reservoir of clear water somewhere up in it to run out in a minute or so and make a light spot in the wash. Load your brush pretty full, not so full that there is danger of spilling the load, and run it along the line which represents, let us say, the ground level at the sides of the building.

Following a Line. *Be sure the wash exactly touches the line* and neither falls short of it, leaving a little light streak, nor overruns it, making it look fuzzy. *This is absolutely essential to a perfect result,* and *I wish I might repeat this warning on every page for every wash.* Also: *Keep the wash evenly wet.*

The brush may be run from left to right, which a right-handed person would call "pushing" the wash, or from right to left which would be "pulling" it. Whichever is the most natural and easiest. When you are sure the wash touches the line throughout its length, widen it either by strokes from side to side or by moving the brush toward you.

Keep the wash evenly wet.

When it is an inch or two wide, do the same on the opposite side of the drawing, and while laying this second wash, break off occasionally and freshen up the edge of the first wash to prevent its drying or making a streak where the ink or pigment in it may settle. Go back to the first wash and widen it another inch or so, and then bring the second wash to the same level. Add a little ink from the godet to the wash you have been using, and widen the washes at right and left alternately as before. Keep darkening the working wash in the godet by putting the *same quantity of Mother Wash* from the other godet into it every two, three or four inches depending on the size of the building and the height of the drawing. It is entirely unnecessary to give one's self the trouble of following not only the outline of the building with its projecting moldings but a border line also. Far better to run over an inked in cutting line and trim the drawing later to that line.

Work quickly, but at the same time with a certain deliberation, not hastily and nervously but with swift, not sudden, movements. Keep your mind alert and develop the faculty of watching all parts of your wash while working. The end you begin on is the one which will dry first if you have made your wash evenly wet. Float these big washes just wet enough to keep wet till you have finished them. It is a great mistake to run them too wet. Also, train your hand to be as light as a feather so that your brush *doesn't touch the paper but only the edge of the thin film of wash*. This is of the utmost importance in the use of heavy deposing pigments. The tiny particles of color are settling down evenly on the paper and the brush disarranges them and makes the wash look muddy. The reason why it is a mistake to run an India Ink wash very wet is very simple. When the wash is run too wet the little particles of ink are floated off to the edges of the wash and dry in a little hard black line; it is also much harder to control the degree of wetness throughout the wash; it is also harder to gauge the amount of water to be taken up in the brush when you have to renew the supply in it; also it is very difficult to follow a line with a wash so wet that it forms, by capillary action, a little bank all along its edges and which the least incaution will spill over the line.

Mending Edges. If properly done, your wash when dry will show a perfect gradation from very light, almost white, to a darker tone at the top of the drawing. Give it time to dry to a point, where, when the backs of the fingers are touched to it it is barely perceptibly damp. Now examine the edges of the wash against the building and ground lines; if they fall short of or run over the line, take a small brush, No. 4 or No. 5 (an old one is best), and wet it a little with clean water, and gently dampen the edges of the wash in these places, blotting them with a fresh clean white blotter until all traces of an overrun and until the little sharp edge of the wash where it falls short are absolutely removed. The reason for going over the edges and mending the bad places at once is because they are much easier to fix up as you go along while the washes are pale and therefore makes a better job. When a wash just touches a line, the line and the edge of the wash are one clean cut line. When it falls short or overlaps and dries, there is, as described, a little sharp dark edge. If this is not removed before the next wash goes on, this little dark edge simply gets darker until it can't be gotten rid of and instead of value meeting value as in Nature, a messy, ragged slovenly edge prevents the values from meeting, destroys the illusion of light and space and air and you are conscious merely of paint and paper and bad workmanship.

Subsequent Sky Washes. Lay another wash exactly as you did the first, throwing away the wash you last used, and starting again with fresh water faintly toned. Repeat all this process including fixing up the wash against the building until the sky is the value you have decided upon. If it has a perfect grade without streaks, thank your stars. If it hasn't, it must be made perfect before you go any further.

Carbonaceous Washes. But before fixing it up the reason for laying this sky wash or any wash in this seemingly laborious way must be explained. Every time you try a short cut you get dead, carbonaceous, non-luminous tones. Assume you have a dark shadow or any dark value in your drawing. If you try to reach it in one, two or four dark washes when you should build it up with eight or twelve or more pale ones, the odds are the result will be dead. A dark wash is infinitely harder to grade than a pale one, and run-backs, streaks and fans are common incidents in its history. A value built up patiently with many pale washes is transparent and luminous and beautiful. It is also a safe method—and there is little common sense in letting a moment's impatience ruin hours of previous effort. But the principal reason is transparency and luminosity.

Imperfectly strained ink is another cause of a carbonaceous quality.

Repairing Defects. Suppose this sky wash or any wash is imperfect, perhaps with streaks in it or darker or lighter areas in it. If it is very bad, the best thing to do before attempting any other remedy is to take a big, soft sponge, tip the board to about 30° with the horizontal and beginning at the light part of the wash, carefully and softly sponge it down, getting as much color off the paper as possible. It is not only not necessary to wait until the whole wash is built up to final value to do this, but it is highly desirable to do it the moment it begins to show defects. When the paper has gone back flat again and dried out until it feels barely damp to the backs of the fingers, set it up in a strong light and examine it critically from a distance and from nearby. If the dark streaks still remain and are pretty bad, the spaces between the streaks must be darkened so that the streaks won't show, or if that is impracticable, the streaks may be turned into the semblance of long thin clouds. This latter expedient is dangerous to resort to, because you are engaged in the presentation of a definite composition which, if sensitively balanced, may be thrown out by such extraneous adjuncts. There is to be sure no excuse for very bad streaks if you are building up a value with pale washes. But faint streaks are frequent and occasionally, by some accident, a greasy spot where a finger tip or whatever has touched the paper makes a light area. These may be equalized by stippling or hatching.

Stippling and Hatching. Take an old brush which has had the point worn blunt if you stipple, and a sharp pointed No. 4 or No. 5 if you cross-hatch, mix up a little very pale wash in a godet, wet the brush in it and soak out almost all of it by touching it to a blotter for an instant, and, with this almost dry brush, dab or hatch, as the case may be, carefully all over the spot. Be particularly careful as you approach the edge of the streak or spot not to lap over on to the dark which you would be merely making darker if you went over it. Let the place dry (or go on to another place if there is one) and then go over it again and again with the same wash and gradually your patience will be rewarded by seeing the bad places entirely disappear and the wash assume an even gradation. If then the whole wash needs to be darkened to bring it up to value, float more washes as originally. Air-brush or atomizer skies are harder to mend but a combination of cross-hatching or stippling, with a careful application of the air-brush or atomizer to give the speckle, will remove practically every trace of trouble.

PLATE 3

BY BIRCH BURDETTE LONG

Mr. Long considers this one of his best drawings and the writer concurs. The problem was to make a drawing in full color in a very high key which would nevertheless have strength enough for purposes of reproduction. The foliage was therefore done in autumn tones, very light and luminous and which, photographed without a screen, has a much darker value in the reproduction than in the drawing. The sky is stippled. (See p. 43.)

When there is time, I believe in laying two or three washes as carefully as possible and then sponging off, laying a couple more and sponging off again. The effect is to soften the tones immensely; they seem to be *in* the paper, not upon it, and to be light and air rather than washes of India Ink. This sponging-off method is especially applicable to detail renderings and will be treated of under that category also.

A wonderful sky may be produced by laying a couple of washes as originally described, sponging off, and laying a couple more, and responging. Then with the old blunt brush nearly dry, and light ink, begin stippling with dabs, not stabs, straight across the top of the sky in a band one to three inches wide; add water to the ink to effect the gradation as you come down, a couple of inches at a time. If it isn't dark enough, go back and do it again but stipple out uneven places first. If well done, this gives a sky with vibration in it, an effect of air and space which is extraordinary.

An Alternate Method of Laying a Sky. For those who find it difficult to keep two washes going at once, there is another method of laying a sky wash which may be noted. It is applicable chiefly, however, to drawings which are divided in the middle for a considerable part of their height by a dome cr tower or the like and in which the sky is assumed to be darkest at the horizon. Mix a good quantity of your wash of the depth of tone you want, pour an equal quantity into two godets of the same size, one of which you set aside. Turn the board around, and, beginning at the ground line, run a wash on one side of the drawing only, grading out from dark to light as you go by adding water at definite intervals, until you reach the top of the dome or tower at the middle, by which time the wash must be diluted to a very pale tone. Thereafter, instead of continuing up the center, carry the wash out in a long diagonal over the top part of the sky in the other half of the drawing. Then blot off the edge of this long triangle softly, or sop it up with a pad of absorbent cotton. Duplicate this process on the other half of the drawing and repeat as necessary until the value you want is established. The laps, if properly executed, are impossible to detect.

Preserving the Brilliancy of the Drawing. It may occur to you to wonder why, if the sky is lighter than the building, we do not run the sky wash over building and all and save a lot of trouble. This may frequently be done, particularly in small drawings where the area to be covered by the wash is therefore quickly covered and you may get back at the building with a blotter before the wash dries and blot it up to practically white again—or, in comparatively unimportant drawings where you are willing to sacrifice brilliancy and perfection to expediency. But although in Nature the tone of a light building is darker than the sky, this is its *general* tone. It has many spots or bands in it of a much lighter value and to render these truthfully and successfully, it is of the utmost importance to save the paper white until you come to these things in their course and then you can make them the value they should be. Again, frequently for the sake of brilliancy it is necessary to leave some parts of the building, some detail perhaps, entirely white, the pure white of the paper being the highest and most brilliant light we have at our command. Just here it may be observed that we often must make our lights lighter and our shadows darker to attain brilliancy in a black and white or monotone drawing than we would in free work or in full color, because we are denied resources in monotone upon which we may draw in full color. A pale violet shadow on a comparatively pale yellowish or orange wall may be made, by just the right choice of tones, to fairly sing and yet be light. It is this brilliancy we have to translate into black and white, and which we get by dark darks and light lights —in short, by strong contrasts.

Dark Horizons. Of course, under certain conditions of weather the sky appears darker near the horizon; also in cities where there is smoke in the air. This is an effect we may legitimately reckon with. Some men like the sky wash to be darker at the bottom to throw the general value of the building up as seen against it—make the building lighter than the sky in other words.

Distances. If there is a background of trees or buildings, it is well to pass several washes over them before putting on the sky washes so that they will be seen softly through the latter. A very good way indeed is to float a wash on these distant forms, let it dry, and float a sky wash, put another wash on them and then another sky wash and so on until you have reached the relative value you wish each to have. The reason here is that whenever you pass a wash over the edge of another wash you slightly soften that edge by washing off some of the particles forming the sharp, crisp edge in which an India Ink wash dries on dry paper.

Combined Gradations. A combination of the dark horizon wash graded up and the sky wash graded down is very often effective. The dark horizon wash would represent a murky, smoky distance beyond which the great dome of the sky goes down. There may be objects like trees or buildings in the distance or this wash itself may form the background. Objects give more interest to the drawing. In this case either put in

the objects first and build up the dark horizon wash over them
or build the two up together. But to get the effect we are discussing you will grade the dark horizon wash very swiftly out
to clear water in the space of a very few inches; or, it is safer
to start with clear water at the point at which the murkiness
is to disappear into the sky and add the murk as you come down
to the horizon. Then turn the board around and run your sky
washes as before. You may also stipple the dark horizon wash
on.

Convention versus Realism. Just here is a good place to
sound a warning against attempting too much realism in an India
Ink drawing of an elevation. You are presenting a design in a
conventional way, not painting a landscape. You only need to
suggest a background in order to locate the building at some
point in space and avoid the appearance of its being suspended
somewhere in the air or built on the edge of the world with
nothing nearer than Jupiter behind it. A compromise drawing
is never a true success. I have tried realistic backgrounds time
and again with geometrical drawings, sometimes in monotone,
sometimes with a good deal of color, sometimes in practically full
color; but somehow the geometrical quality of the elevation was
always inharmonious with the attempted realism of the rest. I
have come to believe that the simpler and more conventional the
accessory backgrounds which appear at the sides of the building,
the better. Attention is then concentrated on the building which
is the occasion of your rendering the drawing. The same is
true of foregrounds. The simpler the better. Some men put
the foreground slightly in perspective and indicate objects in
perspective at the sides of the building. But unless it be done to

express some special relation of the building to the site, it is better, I think, to dispense with perspective.

Sprayed Skies. Since the introduction of the air-brush, sprayed skies have become very popular. They are undeniably beautiful when well done by an expert. They usually err on the side of airlessness and unreality. As a rule they are merely dark curtains hung up behind the building. The atomizer sky is not nearly so successful. The spray is not so fine nor it is uniform, some of the drops of color being much larger than others and falling on the paper in little splashes.

Templates. To spray on a wash, make an accurate tracing of the outlines of the building which should include those of any object or portion you do not wish covered by the spray. This tracing may be used as the template itself or the outline may be transferred to a piece of detail paper. Some use one, some another. This outline should then be carefully cut out with a sharp knife or scissors, or both, and laid over the drawing so that it accurately coincides everywhere. Then with some very fine needles, pin this template you have made at frequent intervals along its edge. Be very careful to hold down all corners thoroughly, both exterior and interior. Then put some weights on the template here and there and spray on the sky. There are certain parts of a drawing, such as a plan of grounds at small scale and the like, for which it is impossible to cut templates. It is the custom in Mr. Goodhue's office to paint such places with rubber cement. This is quite thick and should be diluted with benzine. It is painted on with a brush and after the necessity for covering that part of the surface is past, the cement may be carefully peeled off, leaving the original tone.

I have never tried this but it sounds interesting and entirely feasible.

Air Brushes. Directions come with the air-brush apparatus, of which there are two principal varieties—those run by compressed air supplied in heavy metal cylinders, and those in which you compress the air in a reservoir with a foot treadle as you work.

Atomizers. If you use an atomizer, it is best to get one with a metal nozzle. Those made for spraying the nose and throat are the best. It is amazing how fast the liquid as it passes through the orifice under the pressure of air behind it will wear the hole larger in a hard rubber nozzle. And when that happens, it coughs and splutters and the color comes out in large gobbets. Fill the glass reservoir with water and work the bulb until the nozzle is perfectly clean. Then put your ink or color in the reservoir, filling it about two-thirds full, tilt the nozzle up, point it away from the drawing, from which you stand well away, and squeeze the bulb not too hard but quickly so as to establish an air pressure in the reservoir. When you do this, the spray comes out in a continuous veil, not a series of jets. As soon as the continuous veil is established swing the nozzle back so that the spray falls on the drawing. You stand well away from the drawing so that the larger and heavier drops of water which will fall more quickly than the lighter spray, will fall on the template and not on the uncovered portions, while the fine mist goes on and falls gently on the latter. It should fall as nearly vertical as possible which is the reason for tilting up the nozzle. When the spray is driven against the paper from an angle, it forms, not tiny round dots, but long splashes like exclamation points. Use light ink and build up your value gradually, also the gradation of the wash, which is controlled by blowing more on where you want it. It is well to spray for a while and then let dry, spray again and dry again; otherwise the tiny drops get together and form bigger drops and these in turn small puddles. Impatience in rendering is the surest road to failure. The use of alcohol for thinning the spray wash is said to make a finer spray which dries quickly and avoids some of those troubles. But it is harder to get off than a water spray.

You will find it necessary to watch your template all the time. The color may collect along its edge or run under it on to the drawing. It is sure to buckle with the spray bath it gets. And where the edges lift between the needles, the little hump in the template protects the drawing just enough to prevent the spray from fully covering it. Even the needles will make light streaks if the spray is not falling pretty vertically. To avoid some of these pitfalls, change your position frequently and shoot the spray from different angles. And place thin heavy weights along the edge of the template to hold it down. I prefer detail paper templates. Tracing paper becomes sopping wet in no time— and if you are called away in the midst of the job, by the time you get back it has dried and shrunken away from the edge. With the best of care, when you take off the template you will probably find places where the template was either short or full or had shifted and either the background does not come up to the building or the building has gotten a dose of spray. Mend the background by stippling, or, if you have the courage and the confidence, cut a long slit in a piece of paper the exact shape and size of the place and blow on some more spray. This takes great skill and judgment. The spray on the building is very difficult to get off. Even the slight force of the impact of the tiny drops on the paper seems to drive the ink into it. But off it must come. Soften it up by moving a brush quite full of water over it, blot off the water after the place has had a chance to soak, and with a damp brush and a blotter work at it until it comes out. If it is very stubborn, let it dry thoroughly, and then go at it with a Ruby rubber very gently. Of course, the rubber, and frequently the washing with a brush, will take out some of the lines of the drawing which must be patched up again.

Run-backs. In grading a wash, if, when you recharge your brush, you take up too much fluid, whether pure water or wash, so that the new portion of the wash is wetter than the portion laid just before recharging, you will almost invariably get a run-back or fan; that is to say, the new fluid will spread back into the old part of the wash. This is very apt to happen in very small washes, as when you are grading the washes in windows, which should start dark and be graded out very rapidly to light. It merely takes practise and experience to determine exactly how dry or how wet your brush must be *at all times.* This is one reason for tilting the board. The angle at which the board is tilted by different men is usually an indication of their preference for very wet or quite dry washes. The wetter the wash, the more the board has to be tilted to avoid run-backs.

Don't let the last of a big wash collect in a long puddle at the foot of the drawing as it will by mere force of gravity. Dry it up by running a dry brush along it *outside* the drawing proper, squeezing it out, and when the puddle is almost gone dry it up thoroughly with blotting paper and *watch it* so that it won't collect again.

Damp Weather. When you are rendering a big drawing,

pray for rainy weather.   Washes run well on damp days; on hot
dry days they dry too fast for comfort.

Removing Blots.   Accidents will happen to the most careful man, and sometimes a large drop of color will spatter or fall
on a part of the drawing already rendered.   When this happens,
blot it up instantly but carefully so as not to spread the area
of the blot, and then be patient and wait until the spot is absolutely bone dry.   Take an elderly brush with a blunt point, wet
it somewhat with clean water and pass it very lightly over the
blot a number of times, blotting off every few seconds.   Don't
keep this up too long or you will make the surface of the paper
fuzzy.   Let the blot dry out again and renew the operation.
If it is not very bad, it will usually yield to two or three
treatments.   If it is a really bad one, get it as pale as you can
with the brush, water and blotter and let it dry out absolutely.
Then take a Ruby rubber and very, very gently erase the spot,
especially around the outer edge so that it will be easier to blend
the place into the surrounding wash.   It is not always necessary
to go clear down to white paper, merely till it shows as a *light*
spot in the wash instead of a dark one and this you then patch
as described on page 42.

The Hopeless Stage.   At a certain stage, any water color
drawing, whether in India Ink or full color, looks to the beginner absolutely hopeless.   This is merely because the experience
is lacking which enables him to look beyond the moment to the
finished result.   One of these moments in an India Ink drawing
comes when the general tones are established on the building,
and the washes are laid in the windows and the principal openings and before any shadows are put on.   It looks hopelessly
flat and thoroughly discouraging.   In free work in water color

it comes just before one begins to put in the various little accents and shadows which model the objects and give life. These are moments for the exercise of not merely courage but cool-headedness. It is at times like these that the beginner is apt to lose his head and begin to be foolish and instead of following out the definite set of steps he had planned, become confused and do the wrong thing first, and very soon the drawing is in ripe condition to sponge out and start all over again. The experienced renderer always sees the final result toward which he is working and holds it firmly in his mind, so firmly that he is frequently surprised when kind visitors draw his attention to something he had not yet reached, as being out of value "or not just right." Subconsciously the renderer knows it is not just right but it doesn't bother him; he sees beyond it. He would be quick to see it in another man's drawing—but not in his own until he is ready to see it.

Plane Values. Our sky wash is successfully completed and the building is in pure white against it. The sky looks darker than you thought it would and wanted it to be. Don't worry! It will look lighter when you get something else on the paper. The next process is to establish the relation of the planes of the building to the sky and to each other. Here again let us have recourse to Nature. Looking out of doors we see that on buildings far off the shadows are much lighter and softer than those on buildings nearer at hand. More than that, the relative contrast between the shadows and the color of the distant buildings (their "local color") is not the same as on those across the street—it is not so great.

At this point there are two programs we may adopt. We may either make the local color of the distant buildings light (and when I say distant buildings I mean distant planes; in rendering we think in terms of planes) and their shadows correspondingly light and make the other planes, as we come forward, darker and their shadows correspondingly dark. Or we may make the more distant planes the dark ones and as we come forward make the nearer successively lighter. In the latter case we keep the distant shadows softer and lighter and the nearer shadows successively darker; this gives the utmost brilliancy on the nearer planes because we have here the greatest contrasts between light and shade. This latter of these two systems makes, I think, the more sunny and brilliant drawing. Let us assume that we have decided upon the latter method. This will make the auditorium wall the darkest of the planes of the building, the two side wings next darkest and the central motif the lightest because farthest forward. So much for the building. But how about the balustrade out in front? Here we encounter one of the conventions of rendering in monotone in which effects of relief and of distance are obtained by contrasts. We want to concentrate the interest in the central motif. To do that it must exhibit the greatest brilliancy, therefore the greatest degree of contrast, the highest lights and the darkest relative darks. We can hardly then make the balustrade lighter than the central motif even if it is nearer to us. We therefore bid Nature *au revoir* at this point and embrace a convention by making the balustrade the ·darkest plane we have. An entirely justifiable departure, inconsistent though it seem.

The other seeming inconsistency in making the more distant planes the darker ones is explained by this same matter of brilliancy of contrast. We may bring objects forward by flooding them with light (which is what we have decided to do here) and we throw a veil of atmosphere between ourselves and the planes further off, or rather a series of veils as the planes recede, by passing tones over them shutting off more and more light.

If we had adopted the convention first stated, with the most distant planes the lightest, and the principal plane the darkest, then, in order to make the balustrade stand forward we would make it lighter than the principal plane behind it.

Passing the First Plane Wash. We mix up a very, very pale wash and pass it over the entire building. If the building is long and low it will be better to start at one end and go straight across from top to bottom in one band rather than attempt to lay such a long wash from end to end of the building.

This wash *(and this principle applies to every wash you lay, no matter how large) should still be perceptibly damp when you have finished it.*

Carrying the Wash Out to the End. Most beginners, and indeed some others, do not seem to realize the importance of carrying all washes out to the very end, even though they are so light at last that they seem to be clear water. No matter how large or how small a wash may be, nor how quickly it grades from dark out to nothing, keep on carrying the wash over the whole area to be covered. For instance, you may be building up a graded wash on the wall back of a colonnade. This may grade from very dark at the top to very light at the bottom or vice versa. I have seen men, as soon as the wash was graded out to almost clear water, dry off their brush and give a few dabs along the edge to fade it out, sometimes even blot it up with the heel of the hand or a handkerchief or a blotter. This is bad workmanship and if done a number of times in the same area, results in building up all sorts of little streaks under the wash which give an indescribably dry and mean and mealy appearance. Remember this about India Ink: That one drop in a pint of water will stain that water just enough to modify the color of white paper and by passing a wash of this stained water many times over the same spot, you will build up a surprisingly dark value. It is for this reason that washes must be carried out to the very end and even when they seem, by that time, to be composed of clean water.

The Relative Illumination of Planes. The accompanying diagrams illustrate a matter which must now be considered—the relative illumination of planes.

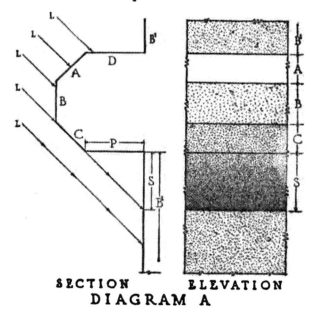

SECTION   ELEVATION
DIAGRAM A

Referring to Diagram A it is evident, with the established geometrical convention that the rays of light are falling at an angle of 45°, that Plane A will be the most brilliantly illuminated because it receives the full power of the light rays L, L, L. They strike Plane B and Plane B ¹ a glancing blow, as it were, and if we could see Plane D we would find it illuminated in the same degree as B and B^1, each of which being parallel and close to each other we may assume to receive the same amount of light. Plane C is not illuminated at all and is therefore in "shade"—not in shadow. That portion of B^1 coresponding to the projection of the lower edge of C beyond the face of B^1 is in shadow—the shadow cast by Projection P. Besides the direct light falling on the object there is another kind of light from other directions—reflected light. But this we will take up in its place. We are now merely studying the planes preliminary to establishing their values with washes and so preparing them to receive shadows. It is evident then that vertical planes are by no means the most brilliantly lighted. The pitches on the tops of cornices, string- and base-courses, steps and platforms and the like correspond in their degree to Plane A. (Also, if we turn the diagram around and look at it as a plan instead of a section we see that if we had a polygonal form such as a tower, the left hand face A would be brightest, B and B^1 which directly face us would be next, and C would be in shade.) These pitches must therefore be left lighter than any other part of the building—each of course in relative value to those planes of the building on which they occur. That on the cornice of the auditorium wall which is furthest back will be in relation to the value established for that wall—which is Plane B modified in brilliancy by distance, the effect of distance being produced by lowering the brilliancy of the white paper by passing washes over it. Therefore it is self-evident that the pitches on the central motif will be the most brilliant of all—the pitches, and the high lights on the columns which correspond to Plane A as a plan, as we have seen.

Building up the Plane Values. Float a second wash over the whole drawing leaving out the Planes A in the central motif. Then a third over the whole of the side wings and auditorium walls. A fourth over the side wings and auditorium leaving out the Planes A in the wings. A fifth over the whole auditorium wall and a sixth leaving out Planes A on this latter. (Page 34.)

By so doing you have established all of these planes in *relative* values and the values of all "A" surfaces to all "B" surfaces in all of the three planes of the building. This does not necessarily mean that the plane of the wings now seems to be enough back from the central motif, nor that the auditorium wall is in its correct relation to either. You have merely established *a* value. You get the true values, which will express the truth of your building in plan, by merely extending this principle and multiplying washes until the values are right.

This is the rendering of plane values in a nutshell. It is applicable to all rendering and all planes. Whenever you are puzzled, recall the principle and everything becomes clear.

Curved Surfaces. Curved surfaces may be considered as merely polygons with an infinite number of sides instead of the semi-octagon given in the diagram. You have but to apply the principle and you will see how any curved surface is lighted, whether cylindrical like a column, spherical as in a dome, or compound as in an ogee. Suppose you have a surface, a section through which cannot be struck with a compass but is perhaps a parabola. Merely divide the surface into a large number of small planes and compare the figure with the simple semi-octagon and you will see at once which are the lightest, which the intermediate, and which the darkest. Once master this principle and nothing can stump you.

Intermediate Subordinate Planes. We have assumed "some columns" with the central motif. We have assumed further that they are *in antis* and that the entrance door is in a wall a few feet behind the columns. This wall will give us a plane intermediate between the principal plane and the face of the side wings of the building. Upon this plane we pass washes sufficient

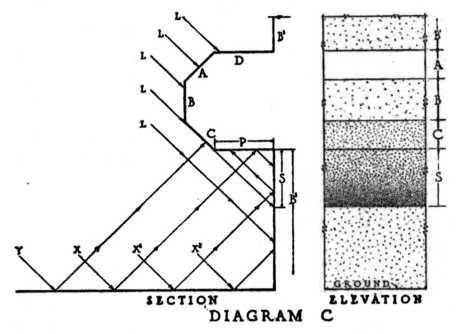

SECTION   ELEVATION
DIAGRAM C

in number to establish its relation to the other planes. For the time being we leave the balustrade as it is. In fact, since it is to be so dark anyway, we have included it in the washes passed over the side wings and it is at present of their value.

Before we proceed to lay shadow washes we must understand the principle of reflected lights and shadows.

Reflected Light. Here in Diagram C is our octagonal arrangement of planes again, with a ground plane and some addi-

tional light rays, from which it will be seen that we must reckon
with more than one source of light—the brilliant light of the sun
coming down from the left and striking some plane like the
ground plane and rebounding against the object with a somewhat diminished brilliancy—diminished because part is lost by
absorption. Examine the course of the Ray X which strikes the
ground, rebounds, hits the underside of P and bounces off on to
Plane B¹ in that portion of it covered by S which is the shadow
cast by the Projection P. Assume Ray X to be merely the central

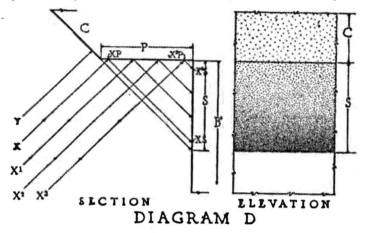

DIAGRAM D

ray of a group. It is evident that these rays as they are reflected
from plane to plane will materially modify the value of the
Shadow S. Also that the brilliancy of the reflected light dimin-
ishes in proportion to the distance of the reflecting plane from the
plane which receives the reflection. To make this clearer we
will enlarge the "P" and "S" part of our diagram.

Ray X strikes nearest the outer edge of P and therefore when
reflected from P strikes nearest the lower edge of the Shadow
S (the angle of reflection being always the same as the angle of
incidence). X³ strikes as shown. X³P to X³S is a much shorter

distance than X-P to X-S and the intermediate rays are also shorter and longer in their proportion. Therefore the reflected light is stronger in the neighborhood of X^2P and X^2S than in that of X-P and X-S. Hence the upper part of the Shadow S nearest to P is lighter than the lower part. We also observe that Ray Y and its group strike Plane C, the effect of which is to lighten it. If the ground plane or reflecting surface were assumed to be at a very great distance, there would be so little reflected light as to be negligible.

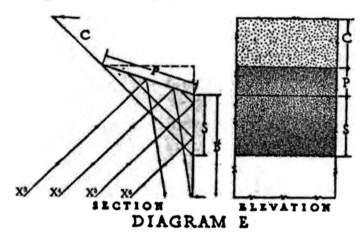

SECTION   ELEVATION
DIAGRAM E

Now let us modify the diagram a trifle by tilting P somewhat so that we may see it in elevation.

Rays X^5 and X^6 are part of the same group of rays which we have observed as being reflected up into the triangle formed by P and S and a line joining their extremities. This group and an infinite company of others we do not show, strike Plane B^1 both inside and outside of the Shadow Area S and are reflected up against P so that instead of being very dark and flat it becomes luminous and has a luminous gradation, the outer portion near C being darkest and that nearest B[1] the lightest, for the same reason that has been given for the gradation of S.

In rendering, all shadows (and indeed all planes) should be graded—and these diagrams furnish the explanation. Before taking up reflected shadows, let us go a little further with reflected light while we are about it, with special reference to two aspects of it—reflected lights in vertical shadows and the grading of planes. (See Diagram F.) Reflected light is as-

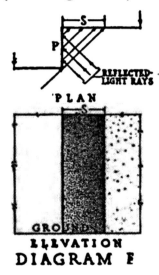

DIAGRAM F

sumed to come from the Right, so that the reflected-light rays, acting as we have previously seen, would make the portion of the vertical shadow nearest P the lightest and there would be an even gradation from the right-hand side of this shadow to the corner at the junction of P and S in plan.

Besides this gradation there is another, from the top of S in elevation to the bottom at the ground line, caused by the reflected light rays from the ground striking into the Shadow S most strongly at the bottom and of course with diminishing force the further from the ground they have to travel. So that such shadows are lightest in their lower part. All this may be very beautifully seen on the southerly front of the Sub-Treasury Building at the head of Broad Street in New York on a sunny day.

If the intensity of shadows is modified and lightened by reflected light as they approach the ground or *any plane approximately parallel thereto,* by the same token so are the values of planes. For the sake of simplification at that moment I did not refer to any gradation of the washes on the planes of our building. But they will have been graded washes.

Some men like to grade their planes from the bottom upwards (a convention I may say which really means the assumption of a darker local color on the lower portion of a building such as the greater accumulation of dirt near the ground) and others down. By the first method, the contrasts at the cornice line are very brilliant—dark shadows on a light surface. Some men grade their planes downward so as to simulate the reflected light from the ground, strengthen their cornice shadows proportionately to get brilliancy against the darker upper surface—and handle the gradation of their reflected shadows and their piquage so as to restore apparent balance and stability to the structure. For if a drawing of a building is lightest next to the ground the building seems to have no satisfactory base and to float. But we are anticipating, as the old-fashioned novelists used to say. (See *Piquage,* pages 78 and 79.)

Either of these methods is sound. One is applicable to certain circumstances and the other to other cases. I think, however, that if our planes are darkest near the ground, we should, to establish a balance in the drawing, reverse the gradation in

such planes as the wall back of our colonnade *in antis* in our
central motif. The same principle of reversal for balance applies to the other system. If our main planes are lightest near
the ground, a plane such as just referred to should be darkest
near the ground. For when there is such a recessed plane, we
may assume that the reflected light from the ground outside
is strong enough to neutralize the light which is reflected from
the plane forming the floor of the recess and actually to cast

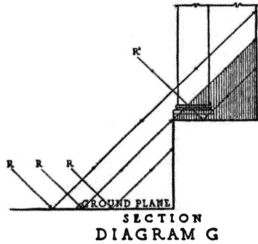

SECTION

DIAGRAM G

the faint reflected shadow of this floor plane which fades out
as it goes up.

In the diagram (G) the group of rays typified by R^1 may
be assumed to be neutralized by the more powerful rays of
reflected light thrown up from the ground, which by a convention we regard as a white reflecting surface for our purpose
instead of a dark absorbent tone.

Reflected or "Back" Shadows. Reflected shadows (which
are colloquially termed "back shadows") are easily understood
once the principle of reflected lights is mastered. If a strong

reflected light is being thrown back upon a plane in shade or in shadow and there should be a projection in that plane, there will be a back-shadow cast by that projection, sometimes fainter than a direct shadow, sometimes quite as sharp, depending upon the relative distance of the shadow-casting object and the light-reflecting plane. (See Diagram H.)

By a convention, into the scientific basis of which it is unnecessary to enter here, reflected shadows or back shadows,

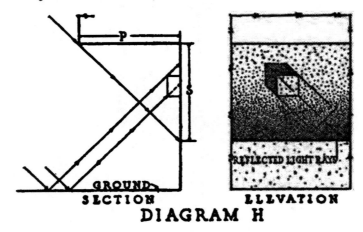

GROUND

SECTION   ELEVATION

DIAGRAM H

are assumed to be cast from some source of light below and to the right, direct shadows being cast from above and the left. Back shadows if large enough to show their gradation in a drawing are darkest nearest the object which throws them and fade out as they go up and to the left.

Reflected shadows are of course constructed in the same manner as direct shadows.

It seems superfluous to enlarge further on the subject of back shadows. The student is advised to examine the illustrations in this book and above all in *D'Espouy's Fragments d'Architecture*. I believe the principles of plane values and their gradation, of the illumination of surfaces and of reflected lights and shadows have been stated with sufficient fullness to make their application easy. It would be tedious to attempt to cover every case. In discussing the rendering of detail drawings we will develop some points unnecessary to touch upon now.

Shades and Shadows. Our plane values established we are ready to put in our shadows. And the first thing we encounter is the problem of plane values again—the minor planes this time.

Godefroy, who was rated as a very skilful renderer in Paris a good many years ago, used to start a drawing by laying the cornice shadow first, on pure white paper; not the whole cornice shadow but that portion of the shadow which falls on the frieze (our "S"), and this he made almost black for a large drawing. I assume his theory was that he had then established two values at the extreme ends of the scale—the white paper and this intensely black and brilliant portion of the shadow of the main cornice—and he worked his half tones and quarter and eighth tones in between these extremes. This is not meat for babes. I advise that the beginner lay the sky or background wash first and follow that with washes which establish the local color of the several planes and their relations to each other and to the sky tone. This gets rid of vast areas of white paper and the judgment of values becomes much easier as well as surer. It used to be my practise to lay the principal cornice shadow next after the sky wash, on the Godefroy theory that I was establishing the principal dark, and I usually rendered this main cornice shadow complete before doing anything else. Accumulated experience, however, leads me to believe that this is not so successful as to establish all the big tones first, all the plane values, and all the local color.

Cornice Shadows. After these are estabished it is now my practise to pass a tone over the whole shadow of the main cornice (whether the main cornice is in one plane or is broken by pavilions or by a central motif) and over the shadows cast by projecting portions, and then work up the full value of the main cornice on the principal plane so as to establish a measure of value to work to. This first wash defines the general modeling enough for one to be able to look ahead and visualize the future steps. Let us pass it. It will go over everything which is in shadow. If modillions occur in the cornice which have sufficient projection to catch the light, of course we leave out the modillions. It is best to start at the right-hand end of the building because, where the central motif projects and casts a shadow, this shadow wash you are running has to be carried down over this shadow area without a stop or a break and be graded as it goes. It does not have to be graded on the running stretch of cornice—this gradation is built up as will be presently described. Therefore carry it flat until it meets the sharp diagonal edge of the shadow cast by the central motif and along and down this diagonal for a bit; then take water and grade it out somewhat toward the central motif and down the edge of the diagonal, grading as you go left and down. For you have two things to accomplish—gradation to the left, to express the reflected light from our old friend, Projection P, and a gradation of the whole shadow down, to express the reflected light from the ground. (See Plate No. 4.) As soon as the edge of the shadow where it touches the central motif is dry, carry the rest of the main cornice shadow wash along to the left-hand end of the drawing.

PLATE 4

BY THE AUTHOR

To illustrate the gradation of the shadow of a cornice and a projecting motif.—"a gradation to the left, to express the reflected light from Projection P, and a gradation of the whole shadow down to express the reflected light from the ground." (See p. 66.)

Work wet but not too wet. Follow the lines absolutely. Do not
let the value of the wash vary by taking too much up in your
brush when you recharge it; if you do your shadow will look
like a piece of watered silk ribbon and will seem to ripple or
undulate.

Then go back to the central motif and count the planes in
the cornice shadow.

Suppose it is as shown in Diagram I. We have ten planes
of which five are vertical and five are so inclined that they will
receive reflected light. (At 1-16th scale unless the size of parts
is tremendous we are not concerned with the actual profile of
planes 2, 4, 6, 8 and 10. They are merely inclined planes.)

Plane 2 will be lightest, 4 next lightest, 6 next after 4.

Plane 1 will be darkest and 3 and 5 successively lighter.

Plane 7 and Plane 9 will be brilliant lights of the same value
at this small scale.

But as for the shadow on 7, to get brilliancy and sparkle
and make it stand forward of 5, we make it darker even than 1.
It is nearer than 1 is to the shadow casting form, which is the
lower edge of 9, and is therefore crisper and darker because a
lot of reflected light rays have a chance to get in between the
edge of 9 and Plane 1 and lighten up the shadow.

So is 5 nearer to the shadow-casting form, vertically. But
it is also nearer to the surface P from which a strong reflected
light is thrown on its face. We make 8 darker than 6, maintaining the relation between 5 and 7 and for the same reason.
We have already passed a wash over all these members except
7, the lighted portion of the modillions. At a larger scale we
would have at least seven and usually many more washes to run.
But we may simplify and make 3 and 5 alike and 4 and 6 alike,

the difference between their projections beyond Plane 1 not being very great.

The shadow is to be graded from light at the top to dark at the bottom. By applying what we know of reflected lights and of the relative value of planes, it is evident that 6 will be the lightest plane in the shadow and we have decided to simplify and make 4 like it. We have already passed one light tone over the whole shadow. Let this tone as it is then stand for 6 and 4.

We pass two more washes over 5, the value of which for purposes of demonstration we assume now to be definitely established, and this same depth of wash twice over 1 and 3. 3 is then established at the same value as 5 having had the same number of washes passed over it. We pass another wash over 1 and 2 and two more washes over 1, or we may pass two first over 1 only and the third wash over 1 and 2 which will soften the junction between them.

Whenever we have approached the projection of the central motif we have lightened these washes to express reflected light, particularly Plane 1.

When we have done all this according to the formula given above I do not mean to say that the relative values of all these planes will be correct. I am merely indicating a method by which you may arrive at the values you yourself want—and the depth of the wash you have been using has a lot to do with the result.

An expert can establish these values pretty closely at sixteenth scale with fewer washes and still attain transparency.

For a very brilliant and sunny shadow I advise having Plane 1 a lot darker than the formula would make it. I like a sharp

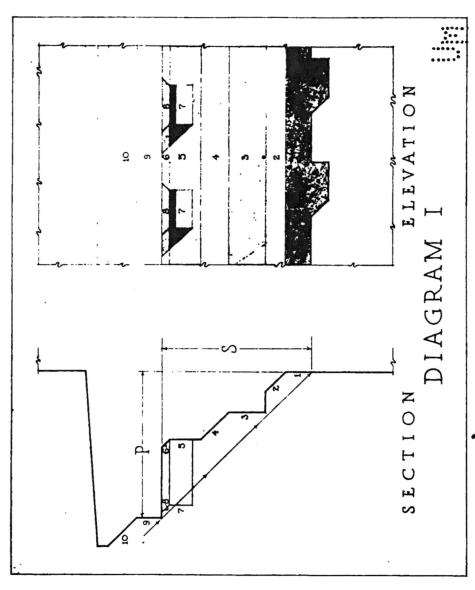

SECTION   ELEVATION

DIAGRAM I

DRAWN BY OLIVER REAGAN

TYPICAL CORNICE SHADOW

To illustrate a typical cornice shadow with the inclined mouldings lighted by reflected light, and the back shadows of the modillions. The values of the reflected lights and of the planes have been simplified, and the relative value of all these planes are not necessarily correct. This is merely an illustration of a method by which the values the draughtsman wants may be arrived at, using a greater number of values and the washes darker or lighter.

gradation between 6 and 1 especially at a small scale where crispness and brilliancy count for more than subtleties of nuance.

Sometimes it is a good idea if the shadow of the modillions is quite long to pass a special wash over the modillion part of the shadow only, fairly dark, and then pass the successive washes for Plane 1 over modillion shadow and all, which will soften the upper edge of the special modillion wash and build the modillion wash up to a darker value than that of Plane 1 by the same operation. The result will be, at a little distance, that Plane 1 will seem to be graded in itself from the lower edge of the modillion shadow up to 2, although you have used perfectly flat tones.

I say "at a little distance." And here let me set up a sign-post of warning. Don't work with your nose to the paper all the time. Keep setting your board up and comparing values and seeing how well what you are doing carries at a distance. Stand away from it. Use a diminishing glass constantly; it flatters in some respects but it condenses areas and values and shows you your defects as well. And as the drawing approaches completion, put it, not in the best light you can find to test its carrying power or beauty, but in the worst light—for in an exhibition or when hung for judgment in a competition it may be hung in a poor light and if you have fooled yourself your labor is lost.

This principle of building up shadows is applicable to all cases. Vertical shadows of course are graded; the gradation is not built up in flat washes. The shadows on planes further back are laid on the same principle but lighter as they go back.

Drawing Back Shadows. We have still to put in the back shadows of the modillions, for which we have prepared by drawing the edges of them with a 5H or 6H pencil very crisply.

This would better be done in two washes, the first to go over both 5 and 6 and the second over 5 only.

The values of these little washes for back shadows and the like are almost in the category of piquage and their strength has to be a matter of experience or judgment. Such washes are of course many shades darker than the first wash you laid in the cornice shadow and which now shows only on 6 and 4.

Colonnade Shadows. Having our whole main cornice shadow rendered, including the central motif and side wings, we may bring the shadows on the wall back of the columns into value. Here we have two options: To grade these shadows from the top down from dark to light, or dark at the bottom and light at the top. If you try the latter, I think you will be pleased with the result, because, when you come to render the capitals of the columns, with crisp, very brilliant little darks, these sharp accents will come against a light background and the greater contrast will give greater brilliancy. Also, the shaded side of the columns will grade from dark at the top to light at the base and the bases will also be quite light, so that you will have the light column bases against the dark part of the shadow, and the shaded side of the column will first show darker against lighter and then lighter against darker as it comes down.

Steps. If there are steps leading up to the central motif, as there probably would be, we may make them recede as they rise, in two ways, first, by passing a tone over the bottom step, then when dry the same tone over the first and second, then over the first, second and third and so on to the top (a variant being to grade them in pairs—one wash on the first two, same wash on these and the next two, the same wash over six, etc.) ; and second, by grading each step by itself and leaving a little sharp light

PLATE 5   BY THE AUTHOR

To illustrate the gradation of tone of a wall behind a colonnade, of the shadows cast by the columns on this wall and the contrast of the dark accents of the column capitals against the lightest part of the wall. (See p. 70.) Also back shadows put in with a ruling pen and the gradation of back shadows. (See pp. 75, 76, 77.)

along the edge of each step and for which we draw light guide lines in pencil to assure the same width to each light edge. These we may start dark at the bottom and grade out lighter, or, we may establish the value we want the top riser to be in relation to the bottom part of the central motif and add value as we go down the steps. And this is the safest and surest way.

Windows. At any time we felt we needed to have their value established to help us with our other values, we will have put the washes in the windows. These should be sharply graded from the top down if the plane they occur in is in full light and from the bottom up if they are in a plane which is in shadow. One wash or more is first put over the whole opening which will represent the color and value of the frame and sash, and subsequent washes over the glass. Frequently the window frame is made darker than the glass and is put in with a ruling pen and the shadow on the frame still darker, almost black. This is purely a matter of taste and of the kind of building we are rendering—its whole character and quality will help to determine such questions of treatment.

Grading Small Washes. There are several ways of grading all small washes and such as we usually get in windows. One is to use two brushes, one of which is loaded with clear water and the other with wash; we start with the wash at the top and carry it down about a third of the height; take the other brush quickly and, leaving a little gap between the wash just laid, run clear water over the rest of the window, then still with the clear water brush, close the gap between the color wash and the clear water by bringing the water up to the color. If the two washes are of exactly the right and equal degrees of wetness the two will flow together and make a beautiful gradation. The brush may be used to guide the fusion. If one wash is wetter than the other, the lighter will fan up into the darker or vice versa.

Another way is to use one brush, lay the upper third of the window, dip the tip of the brush very carefully into clear water and take up exactly enough to make up for what you have just laid on the paper, carry this wash down another third of the way, wash out the brush quickly and vigorously in your big bowl or casserole, take clear water out of another receptacle and grade out with this to the bottom.

Another way is to mix a tone for the top third, another for the second third about a quarter as dark. Lay the top third, wash out your brush thoroughly and recharge it with the second wash, wash it out thoroughly and take clear water for the last third.

Another way still is to take out two brushfuls of the Mother Wash and put them in a godet, lay part of the wash, add a little water in the godet, mixing it thoroughly with the Mother Wash in it, lay some more wash, lighten up again and repeat. Then throw away what is left of your diluted little wash and start over again for the next window; or you may grade from light to dark by adding ink.

Of course these methods are applicable to any wash and the best way is to try them out and see which suits your own temperament; or invent a new way for yourself. Only, it has to be a way you can count upon every time to produce a certain result. In free rendering one often gets a spot of color, a window perhaps, with the most delicious gradations and fusions of color which were the result of working fast and wet and the effect was produced almost by itself—to save your soul you couldn't

repeat just that thing again.   In formal rendering you have to
repeat the same thing again and again and *know how to do it.*

General Warning as to Grading Washes.   There is another thing to guard against in grading washes—a tendency to
run the wash drier as you lighten it.   *All parts of every wash*
must be evenly wet.   When you have finished a wash, the be-
ginning of it should still be perceptibly wet.   And let me repeat
again, no matter how light the wash may be, even if it is pure
water (or seems to be) carry it over the whole area it should
cover.   Don't fade it off with dry brush strokes.

Column Shades and Shadows.   The washes on the shaded
side of the columns are done in all sorts of ways.   Some men
run the brush against a T-square held away from the paper,
slap out the color, take pure water and run it down the edges,
and the streaks blend.   Others run it by hand by a variation of
the window wash method, carrying a narrow vertical band of
the color down a way, taking up water in the brush and going
back to the top and running a second vertical band beside the
first over the rest of the shaded part, and repeating the operation, grading down and sideways in sections as it were, then
passing a general graded wash, darkest at the right hand 45°
point, over the whole column except the high light.

Another but much more laborious way is to build up the
gradation *around* the column (and lengthwise also of course)
by laying a series of bands graded from top to bottom corre-
sponding to the flutes.   An unfluted column may of course be
modeled in the same way.   Diagram J shows how this would be
done on a large-scale unfluted column.   (See page 74.)

For an unfluted column we draw two light pencil lines representing the width of the high light.   And whether fluted or

unfluted (unless we do it as though flute by flute) the shade line at the right-hand 45° point is drawn sharply in pencil. Frequently, in a very light drawing the pencil line itself at the lightest parts of the shade will seem to model the column and

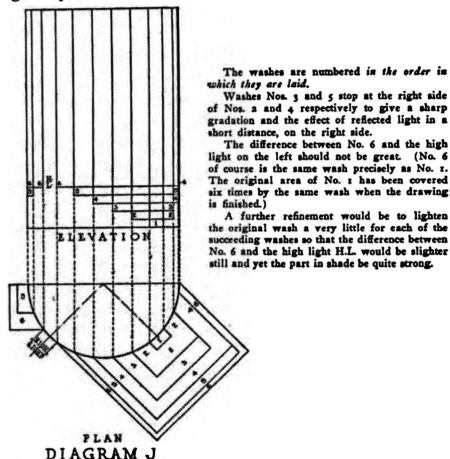

The washes are numbered *in the order in which they are laid.*

Washes Nos. 3 and 5 stop at the right side of Nos. 2 and 4 respectively to give a sharp gradation and the effect of reflected light in a short distance, on the right side.

The difference between No. 6 and the high light on the left should not be great. (No. 6 of course is the same wash precisely as No. 1. The original area of No. 1 has been covered six times by the same wash when the drawing is finished.)

A further refinement would be to lighten the original wash a very little for each of the succeeding washes so that the difference between No. 6 and the high light H.L. would be slighter still and yet the part in shade be quite strong.

DIAGRAM J

seem to define an area of a different value from the rest of it. To make a good job of an unfluted column by the method given in the diagram, very, very light guide lines should be drawn. But unless the columns are colossal, this is not worth while at sixteenth scale. At eighth scale, yes; while at quarter scale if the column has any size at all the treatment is like that for larger scale details. (See Plate No. 8 which is at quarter inch but the monumental scale made it possible to treat it more like a three-quarter inch scale detail.)

Small Shadows. For the crisp little shadow under the necking of the column it is a good idea at sixteenth scale to use a free hand pen dipped in dark wash (perhaps the full strength of the Mother Wash), draw the darkest part of the shadow and make sure it is very wet *without scratching the paper with the pen;* then either with a brush or the pen washed clean, run clear water right and left, close the gaps and the dark ink will flow into the clear water alongside. Column bases may be rendered in much the same way.

Use of the Pen. The shadows of ornament are usually best put in with a free hand pen. Care must be taken not to scratch them into the paper because the fibers then are stained unevenly and the result is messy. A dull pen is best—dull, but of the proper degree of fineness or coarseness for the width of the shadows. Also the shadows of window architraves or of the projecting planes in a classic architrave or the like—any member which projects so little that it is impracticable to use a brush —may be put in with a ruling pen, laid *firmly on the paper without biting the line in,* the pen being opened so as to exactly cover the width of the shadow; *never* build up the width of such shadows by running lines side by side—"painting" them with the pen. This applies to both horizontal or vertical shadows. The horizontal ones are of course the same value throughout. The gradation of a vertical shadow done with the ruling pen is very simply accomplished by touching one end of the line again, load-

ing that part of the line with more color than the rest. This
is applicable also to the shadows or shades of ribs or tiles on
roofs which it is usual to make grade *away* from us (that is,
from dark at the bottom to light at the ridge). The whole shade
or shadow is first ruled in very wet, and then, giving the line
a second or so to dry a bit, start again at the bottom and draw
a short line swiftly, lifting the hand as you go up the old line.
If this should prove inadequate touch the bottom of the line
again to darken it.

Usually the combined width of the shaded side of the rib
and its shadow is sufficiently wide to run with a brush. Therefore a wash representing the value of the shade may be run
over both and the shadow only done with the ruling pen as
described.

Back Shadows and Piquage. One of the last steps toward
the completion of a drawing is putting in the back shadows
which is really a part of the process of piquage. In order not to
complicate an already sufficiently intricate description I have
deferred to this point the question of reflected lights also, because
they are more easily described in connection with reflected or
back shadows. As we have seen in Diagram E planes such as a
cyma, which correspond to the surface "P" in this diagram, are
in shade. When the cornice of which they are a part is in
shadow, they are illuminated by reflected light and by a convention this reflected light is always represented as being a little
stronger than in Nature for the sake of clarity and brilliancy.
In running the wash which represents the shade on such planes,
when we come to the point at which the cyma or other member
enters the shadow, we immediately lighten the wash, usually
grading it out to clear water in a very short distance; and where

these members or the shadows they cast are so narrow as to require that they be put in with a ruling pen, they should be stopped at the edge of the shadow. An examination of some of the illustrations in this book, notably Plate No. 5, will tell more at a glance than a page of description. The same is true of back shadows which may be examined in the same illustrations. You will observe that the back shadow cast upon the frieze by the upper member of the architrave is graded strongly from the outer edge of the shadow area toward the left in Plate No. 5, for back shadows are lightened by reflected light just as direct shadows are.

The casting of back shadows can easily be overdone and it is frequently advisable to omit some altogether. Observe the sculpture in the pediment in Plate No. 4 where, although it has considerable projection, there are no back shadows cast up against the bed moldings of the cornice. They might easily have looked grotesque and confused at a little distance and would not explain themselves to the eye. Very small back shadows, such as those in rustication, are best put in with a ruling pen in the same way that direct shadows of similar width are done.

Back Shades.   Besides back shadows there are also "back shades." We have seen in the relative illumination of planes that inclined surfaces similar to Plane "A" in Diagram A are the most brilliantly illuminated when in direct light. By the same token they are always represented as the darkest value when in a shadow area; so the pitch on top of a cyma or any projecting member or plane is always represented as much darker than the back shadow such a projection would cast. As to the relative value of the back shadows and back shades to the shadows or shades in which they occur, this can only be arrived at by experience. In a small scale drawing they are usually quite narrow and therefore too difficult to build up with a series of washes and so have to be done in one operation, requiring the judgment which comes by practise.

Piquage. A shadow, however transparently laid, may occasionally seem to lack transparency, and strengthening the joint lines in the shadow area invariably helps to make the shadow transparent at once (see Plate No. 9). Up to this point you have passed nothing but general tones over the various planes besides the shadows and the back shadows. The drawing still has a rather papery look. It lacks the look of stone. In Nature the stones in a building usually vary in color or tone and in rendering we express these differences. This is done by passing tones of varying value over individual stones leaving a narrow light line along the top and left-hand end of the stone. It is advisable to *piquer* several stones in a group here and there, each varying in tone. One of the most difficult things to learn about this particular element of piquage is the avoidance of a spotty appearance. It should be done with great judgment and reserve. The little washes on each stone are put on *very wet,* for this is one of the times when you want a wash to dry with a sharp little edge. It is often a good idea to piquer a stone which is partly in and partly out of a shadow. Columns seem to float unless the lower parts of the shaft are darkened and this sort of piquage simulates the weathering which stone work near the ground gets from the spattering of rain. The same is true of the lower part of the building and it seems to stabilize the whole structure if the lowest courses of stone are darkened, grading up to lighter as they rise. Each stone in a course should be *piqué* by itself with slightly varying degrees of wetness so that each one will dry out a little different from its fellow, but the general effect of each lower course must be darker than the course above it. Another element in the process of piquage is to go carefully over the lines of the drawing and examine them with a view to strengthening certain ones here and there to assure firmness, clarity and readability. The shadows of ornament or sculpture and the like are not strictly to be considered as piquage. The effect of a considerable texture on any stone may be produced by dots with a pen. See Plate No. 6 for the rustication on the angles and in the base course. This drawing is reproduced at about full size.

Another part of the process is to sharpen up the lines of frames and sash in window openings and the metal work in wrought iron doors and so on. These latter are usually rendered entirely with the ruling or free hand pen, practically never with a brush.

Brickwork. There are a number of ways to render the effect of brickwork appropriate to the scale of the drawing. At sixteenth scale we indicate rather than draw. At eighth scale things begin to get big enough to realize the greater part of their individual characters while at quarter scale everything should be drawn—really drawn. This always should be remembered, and the treatment of the structural lines, the shadow-casting forms, the shades and shadows and the indications of materials kept in scale with the scale of the drawing. Therefore at sixteenth scale, in monotone, pass a wash over your brickwork which when dry will start with that value which the value of the brick color should exhibit in relation to the stonework, and grade it out fast to quite light. Then with a ruling pen opened to the width of a brick, draw some crisp indications of brick, in scale, using ink of varying degrees of darkness, with a very few very dark for accents. It takes care and practise to do it well. It should not be done all over nor should it (except in the case of the few accents referred to) be too strong in contrast to the general tone of the wash. The beginner will find some difficulty at first in gauging the value of these lines, forgetting, as one does constantly at first, that India Ink dries out many values lighter than when wet.

Use of the Rubber. When we think the drawing is all done and that we have done everything to it we can there is still a good deal which may be done. Sometimes parts of it look dead and need life and light. What to do? The draughtsman's best friends are his rubber and his sponge. We can't use the sponge just now, but we may take a brand new sharp Ruby rubber and delicately lighten what needs lightening. This must be done very carefully or a frightful mess will result. Sometimes a top fillet or a corona needs lightening up to give more brilliancy, sometimes the high lights on columns are not brilliant enough. Use a visiting card with a slit cut in it or a metal erasing shield if you don't trust your hand to do it accurately, unaided.

Sometimes you find with a fresh eye after a good night's sleep that a whole plane is too dark. Even this may be remedied with a Ruby rubber, using the whole long edge which must touch the paper with an even pressure everywhere in a kind of light sweeping movement towards you from right to left if you are right-handed. Here if anywhere does disaster wait upon impatience or lack of care. There is something exciting about anything to do with the use of color which is apt to make men hurry when there is really lots of time. A novice at tennis always hurries his stroke and flubs into the net. It is like that. It

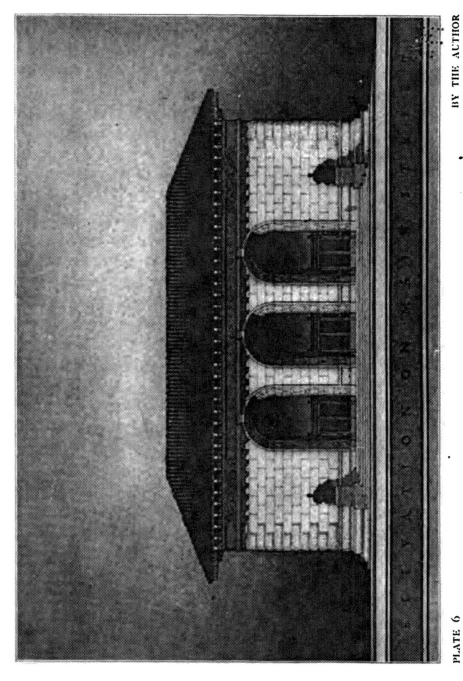

PLATE 6

BY THE AUTHOR

To illustrate texture made by a pen in the rusticated course in the base and the quoins at the angles. (See p. 79.) Also the effect of transparency in the cornice shadow due to back shadows and reflected light.

really takes more patience, more skill, more cool thought and method to touch a drawing up than to make it in the first place.

Darkening Up. Sometimes after you have duly passed washes of the proper value over a plane (which seemed right and were right) and then put in all the darks of the right value, you find some narrow bands of the original plane value staring at you—fairly jumping out at you. This would happen for instance in such a place as where windows occur between pilasters, the shadows of which on the wall leave a rather narrow strip of lighted wall between them and the window-dark. These places must of course be toned down and it is surprising how much toning they need to bring them down to the apparent value of the rest of the plane. The reason of course is that a light imprisoned between two darks always seems more brilliant than it really is—than the tone you made it before you put the darks on.

Textures. Under the head of piquage may properly come the matter of textures. India Ink not being a deposing pigment, the many suggestions of texture we may get with heavy colors are denied us and we have to find other ways to indicate it. For example, trees may have a texture put all over them in any of a dozen ways with a free hand pen and washes then passed over the whole tree modeling the foliage masses, and with the shadows put on crisply or softly, as the plane demands, with the brush or cross-hatched with a pen. (See Plate No. 7.)

Stonework may be stippled with pen or brush and the stippling pulled together with a wash over all. Jules Guérin has for years given texture to an otherwise flat tone by drawing over and through it with a Conté crayon or a black Blaisdell pencil neither of which shines as lead pencil does. In the drawing

(Plate No. 8) the foliage of the tree was completely drawn in pen and ink leaf by leaf and then rendered in wash to give the modeling and the accents.

Body Color. It is sometimes necessary to put in very narrow lights in body color with a ruling pen. It is not always feasible nor worth while to leave out the delicate tracery of a bronze grille which in sunlight would perhaps look best if drawn in light against the dark of the opening, the sash and muntins of windows or the very fine line of reflected light we sometimes put on the upper and left-hand edges of window panes or frames in the shadow part of a window. For this we use Chinese White which we tone or not according to circumstances. It must be thoroughly softened and of a consistency like very thick cream so that it has a lot of body. The pen you use it in must be clean and must be sharp. The Chinese White will dry quite quickly in the pen which must therefore be washed out absolutely clean at frequent intervals else the color will cake and refuse to flow freely. It must issue in a clean crisp line with neither a dry crumbly appearance nor with blobs at the ends. The Chinese White is merely the opaque vehicle for the lighter value you are putting over a darker tone. The thick pigment hides the dark tone, the toning agent you use in it, whether India Ink or color, gives you your value and quality.

PLATE 7   BY BELLOWS, RIPLEY, CLAPP AND FAELTEN

To illustrate a free method of getting texture and rendering the effect of foliage in a formal
drawing. Done with pen, crayon or pencil, and brush. (See p. 81.)

III

QUARTER-, HALF-, OR THREE-QUARTER-COLOR

The drawing we have just carried to conclusion is in pure monotone. It is true that we used pigments to tone the ink—but not enough to count as color. We attained our effects by the sheer relation of value to value.

We have now to discuss the use of color in another way, in which the general effect of monotone is preserved but in which as we examine the various washes we plainly see that pigments have been used. It is an intermediate step between pure India Ink rendering and rendering in full color and is very flexible— for we may use almost no color and yet give great quality to our drawing which remains a monotone, or use so much color that we have to all intents and purposes a drawing in full color. India Ink is still our basic tone. Whistler called black "the great harmonizer." But however questionable its use in painting in oil has since been proved to be, it is indubitably the right base for rendering architectural subjects, formally, in water color.

Warm and Cold Backgrounds. It used to be a formula in the âteliers in Paris that a warm building demanded a cool background and a cool building a warm one. But this does not state the whole case—we may also make the whole drawing warm or make it all cold. The question is purely one of preference (I purposely avoid the word "taste" in this connection). There is one touchstone of success—harmony, the preservation of the key. If the building is singing in A minor and the background in C minor we have a discord. I have found it possible to get a very considerable effect of color with very few pigments and keep the drawing in key. These pigments are Carmine, Vermilion, Raw Sienna, Burnt Sienna, Verte Emeraude, Cobalt Blue and French Blue. These happen to be the ones I fell into the way of using years ago and, liking what they gave me and reaching a point where I know exactly what I can do with them, I continue to use them. It is therefore with this palette of my own that I am about to deal. As you will see, Messrs. Cret and Ripley use quite different combinations and different pigments. (See Properties of Pigments, pages 129-131.)

I find that by varying the proportions of the cool and warm pigments and by changing the speed at which the wash is run, I can get a surprising variety of tone. More than that, by opposing cold and warm tones to each other a soft brilliancy in a light key may be attained. It is unnecessary to visit the coal scuttle for tones to express brilliant light. In Greece, on the Acropolis of Athens, in the Propyleia, the Parthenon, the Erechtheion, the shadows are struck so full of reflected lights as to seem to cease to be shadow and to become merely another kind of light. And it would be a brutal lie to model one of those buildings with strong heavy dark shadows. There was an old party in Rome years ago of whom some of my contemporaries took lessons in water color. He had one recipe for shadows— French Blue and Vandyke Brown—perfectly opaque, with a specious kind of richness about it. A fallen capital with some Yellow Ochre run over it, leaving a few whites for recent fractures, the soup aforementioned for the shadows, and Rome breathed again—or turned over in her grave. This recipe was

PLATE 8   BY THE AUTHOR

To illustrate the fact that monumental scale makes it
possible to treat a quarter-inch scale detail more like
one at three-quarter scale. (See p. 95.) Also the rendering of foliage in a formal drawing (see p. 82), and the
reflected light on the edges of window sash. (See p. 99.)

carried to the Athenian Acropolis and there used and I only wonder that the grey-eyed Athene didn't throw the perpetrators of the sacrilege off the Rock.

Quality. Instead of a mere difference in the *value* of tones we are also to create a difference in their *quality*. Distant planes will not be merely lighter (or darker according to the convention we adopt) but will be colder—indeed the mere difference in quality (which means color, used in this sense) will make one plane recede and the other advance. To illustrate: If we mix two washes of India Ink of as nearly the same *value* as we can, one warmed with, say, Burnt Sienna and the other cooled with French Blue, and lay them side by side the cold tone will seem further off than the warm one.

But we may play cold tones against warm ones and still make them come forward by a *difference* of value. Remember Denman Ross's definition of value—the *amount of light* in a tone. We are not to substitute the *quality of light,* which is color, for value. We are to use them both, keeping our color *in value.*

I have just said that distant planes are colder than those near by. This simply means that there is more air between us and those planes, more space if you will. Look up at the sky on a bright day. The marvelous depth of color you see is merely the depth of interstellar space seen through our thin film of atmosphere. So there is more of this atmosphere between us and the distance. Therefore if we were to make our elevation (Diagram B, facing page 34) all over again using color in our washes, more, or less, according to our aim, we would take out some of the Mother Wash, which in this case may be the pure India Ink, reduce it with water to the value we want and add warm or cold, transparent or deposing pigments to it. The sky washes may be warmed up with Burnt Sienna and Carmine followed by other washes with only Cobalt Blue in them floated or stippled on. This gives a singular effect of cool warmth, if one may so express it, and of atmosphere. Of course the sky is not cold. On a warm summer day, looked at without the prejudice which has grown up in our minds because we have been taught from our cradles that the sky is "blue," it is seen to be full of little particles of red floating in it. And sometimes it is very green. And it changes all day long.

Over the auditorium wall we pass tones in which we have introduced more Cobalt Blue than Burnt Sienna and Carmine (or any other of the toning agents you prefer or elect to experiment with—remember I am speaking in terms of my own palette and general practise). For throughout the drawing, with very few exceptions, there should be both Cold and Warm in every wash, each to preponderate according to its distance. The wings of the building will have less Blue and the central motif almost none. The *value* of the balustrade and steps out in front will still be very strong. But, as one of the exceptions noted just now, it should have no Blue in the wash. You may depend upon the black of the India Ink to hold down the Burnt Sienna and Carmine and keep them from being too hot.

When we run the main cornice shadows we encounter another, and a major, exception. The first washes, which represent the planes or moldings *lighted by reflected light,* have no Blue in them. The other planes have a preponderance of Blue, the darkest and bluest being our old friend Plane 1 in Diagram I. For Planes 3 and 5 in the same diagram we need merely lighten the wash we have mixed for 1 with water. For shadows, I use as a rule, French Blue instead of Cobalt. We must mark an important difference at this point between methods in this and in pure monotone. You are now using a perceptible amount of color, deposing pigments, in your washes. Such washes when very thin and pale, will bear quite a bit of working over without stirring them up, causing the color to "lift" and making the drawing muddy and messy, but the planes in such shadows, for example, as the main cornice and that of the principal motif on the side wings should be put on and left alone, not built up. Part of their beauty will reside in the way the pigments settle out. It therefore requires experience and judgment, and failures conquered by patience and courage to judge accurately two elements —the *value* of such a shadow and its *quality* or color. You are working with two very tricky materials—India Ink which dries out many tones lighter than it looks when wet and deposing pigments like French Blue, for instance, which settles out and dries very much bluer than you'd guess by looking at the wash in the godet. Common sense would point toward experiment before starting boldly in to spoil a perfectly good drawing—and a very good way to experiment is to draw a portion of the building on another piece of paper and use it for your experiments; or you may run some of your wash on the edge of a piece of paper and hold it against the drawing when it is dry to see whether it is the right value and color.

Running Washes Containing Much Color. The mechanical processes of running the washes and grading them out are the same as in working in pure monochrome except that you must be even more careful to keep your wash moving and not allow it to settle in streaks or spots because you have a lot of color in it now, whose whole business in life is to settle and settle quickly.

The voids of windows and doorways may be made warm or

cold as you please. You may assume rich warm curtains behind
the glass if you like—but just remember that more drawings
are spoiled by the character, treatment and quality of the window
washes (if there be many) than in almost any other way. Making a success of it is the touchstone.

Accessory trees and shrubs may have an approximation to
the color of Nature according to the color scale you have adopted
—how near to, or how far from, full color,

Grading from Cold to Warm and Vice Versa. When you
have mastered pure monotone and the variation just described
(which we may call quarter-, half-, or three-quarter-color as it
approaches full), then you will begin to find ways of your own,
as for instance, grading not merely from dark to light but from
cold to warm—dark and warm to light and cold, or dark and
cold to light and warm. Some of the most beautiful effects
in rendering are obtainable by this dodge. The shadows of the
columns on the wall in Plate No. 9 were graded from cold and
dark at the top to warm and light at the bottom where a warm
reflected light was assumed. (Shadow being partly describable
as the absence of light and therefore of warmth, reflected light is
assumed to be warm and gives us our warrant for many beautiful
effects of contrast of warm and cold tones.) The shadow in the
arch is graded down from light and warm at the top where the
reflected light from the intrados is supposed to strike into it,
warming and lightening it, to dark and cold at the bottom.
(Plate No. 9.) And the back shadows are darker and colder
than the shadow proper. This is done of course by mixing two
washes, one cool and dark and the other light and warm, starting
with the cool and using the lighter, warmer wash to grade it out
with at first and then water as necessary.

PLATE 9   BY THE AUTHOR

To illustrate the omission of back shadows of the sculpture in the pediment cornice
shadow. (See p. 77.)
Also the strengthening of joint lines in the shadows of the columns to make them more transparent
(see p. 78), the gradation of the statue and column shadows from cold and dark at the top, to
warm and light at the bottom, and the gradation of the shadow in the arch from light and warm
at the top, to dark and cold at the bottom. (See p. 88.)

Piquage in Color. When you come to piquer your drawing in quarter-, or half-, or three-quarter-color you have many opportunities for producing beautiful general tones by the juxtaposition of small tones of various qualities, reddish, yellowish, greenish, bluish, on individual stones, always laid crisp and wet and *left alone* to dry, not messed with in a panic because they do not seem quite right at first. *Never fool with a wet wash unless you know how.* Picking out certain stones in a warm shadow with cold piquage or vice versa are all finishing touches which it is sufficient to suggest.

Unifying Washes. Sometimes when a drawing has reached a certain point, perhaps is supposed to be finished, the general tone is too hot or too cold or is discordant, has gotten out of hand and out of key. If you haven't time to sponge it 'way down and begin almost fresh, it may often be saved by floating one big wash or more over the whole thing, sky and all. If it is too hot, mix a cool grey as transparent as possible. If too cold *don't float Yellow Ochre over it,* but mix up a wash of warm *transparent* pigments. In so doing you are dealing probably with tertiary colors which are apt to be very muddy and ugly (by tertiary colors is meant the mixture of two secondary colors like orange and green which are the product of the mixture of the primaries red and yellow and blue and yellow respectively), and you must therefore study the quality of the unsatisfactory general tone of the drawing with great care and mix a tone which will modify it beautifully, not make it uglier still. In floating these big unifying washes a light hand is more than ever required. The board should be tilted to about 30° with the horizontal, the largest possible brush used, the wash run as wet as it will stand and yet not run down in streaks, and only the film of wash touched with the brush and not the paper at all. As usual two or three light washes may be better than one—this depends upon the skill and experience of the operator. It will be found necessary as a rule to sharpen up the shadows here and there afterwards to restore some of the crispness and brilliancy which have been lost.

The Glazing Method. There is another way of making a drawing which gives the effect of full color and is applicable to perspectives as well as to geometrical elevations. It is particularly valuable in perspectives in cases where it is essential to preserve the facts of the design, model it perfectly and subtly and yet avoid any suggestion of the formal, dry and precise. A few words will suffice to describe it. Assume the drawing to be in perspective. Observe all the care in the preliminaries and then ink it in with a very fine light line. Sponge it off. Then establish the plane values and put on all the shadows in pure India Ink monotone, all a little stronger than they look as though they should be. Float a sky wash in full color over the whole drawing, background and all. Blot up with a blotter the structure itself but not the background. Mend up edges as in India Ink rendering. Put in such things as human figures in the foreground which should have been carefully composed and inked in with the rest of the drawing. Put in a background in full color. Then float one or two big washes over the building and foreground, which may be warm and sunny at the top, perhaps, and grade down into cool violets.

This is nothing more than an adaptation to water color of the glazing methods of the old masters of oil painting, who modeled their whole painting first in monotone, thus establishing all their values, and then with thin, transparent coats of varnish to which color was added went over it again to give local color. To this was added the further subtlety of glazing again with another color—which resulted in those marvelous tones and effects of light and shade which the moderns have discarded for direct painting, in an endeavor to produce the effect at one stroke and by practically one step and one process. Remembering that in water color painting our shadows are put on last, if we render in full color and we want the drawing to show plenty of texture, we must use deposing pigments; we will lose subtlety of modeling and a certain kind of beauty and delicacy if strong shadows of deposing pigments are put on surfaces already covered with deposing pigment; for almost immediately the color lifts and stirs and the shadows seem to be *cut through* the wash they appear on and look messy. The method described avoids this. The India Ink washes are put on stronger than they look as though they should be before the color goes on because the subsequent washes of color *have more effect upon the light parts of the drawing than upon the darker parts* and therefore tend to draw them nearer together in value. So your contrasts of light and shade must be strong enough to start with to stand a considerable modification.

This scheme has the further advantage of being surprisingly rapid and yet giving an effect of great finesse. And it is very safe for a drawing you are especially anxious to have good and have only a limited time for. I suppose this is partly because the process is resolved into two simple elements, each of which is separately carried out—the establishment of *values* in monotone first, and of *quality* in color afterwards.

Enough perhaps has been said of this phase of the subject. I have said far more than I intended to say when I began. Indeed, had I fairly envisaged the difficulty of clearly describing in words processes which could be demonstrated physically in a moment, I might not have had the hardihood to begin. It would be so much easier to seize a brush and say, "Here! Do it so! You hold the brush like this and you pull the wash so, as fast as this, and you take water this way." We have still to discuss the rendering of sections, of details and of plans and to say something about full color and sketching.

IV

RENDERING SECTIONS

There are two ways of rendering a section; one is to regard it as though it were like a plaster model sawed through and set up in bright sunlight which would cause the cut ceiling solids to cast shadows on the wall surfaces, part of the wall, perhaps, being in full light; the other is to disregard the fact that one wall and a part of the ceiling has been taken away, and to render the interior entirely in reflected lights and shades and shadows. This I think is the better way particularly if the section is taken through court yards open to the sky as well as through roofed-in spaces, for the difference in lighting is then clearly expressed.

Beyond this there is nothing to say except that sections are principally a problem in reflected lights, shades and shadows, that the cut sections may be left white or slightly toned and that the principles laid down for elevations apply in all respects.

V

RENDERING DETAIL DRAWINGS

Once the secret is known, let no one despair who gazes upon those wonderful shadows we see in Corinthian column capitals in *D'Espouy's Fragments d'Architecture* and thinks men who can cast such complicated shadows on broken surfaces a race of supermen one may never hope to equal. In common with hundreds of others I bowed the head in awe and wonderment—until one day I visited the Villa Medici and found that the Grand Prix men are just as human as every one else and do not hesitate to take the easier way when they can. And for all those marvelous shadows in Corinthian capitals and all sorts of other ornamental and structural detail, they simply procure plaster casts, take them out into the sunlight of the Villa gardens and turning the object in such a way that the sun casts shadows from the left at 45° they quickly draw the outline of said shadows with a soft pencil on the plaster cast. Having them there it is a very easy mechanical process to transfer them to paper with the rest of the forms. Observe, however, that while they avoid the painful task of laboriously constructing their shadows, they do deal more with reality than we do in this country. In what school are students made to measure and draw the orders even from plaster casts? In what school do they learn gradation of tones in shadow and the delicate secrets of reflected lights and shadows from an actual object which has three dimensions? None! Everything is copied from other drawings, taken from

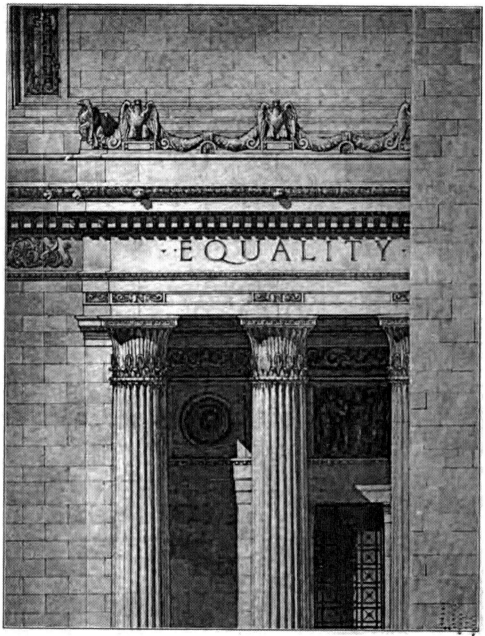

PLATE 10   BY PAUL PHILIPE CRET

To illustrate among other things, the light band along the edge of the great obelisk at the right,
and on the left-hand edge of the main motif. (See p. 97.) Also the piquage of stonework by
texture drawn with a crayon and by the treatment of the joints.

books or is faked up. The Grand Prix man doesn't have to spend his time or risk his neck measuring the actual capital. A cast for his purpose is quite as good, brought to the Villa where he can measure and study it comfortably and where, when he is ready to lay the washes on his drawing, he has it constantly at hand to refer to. In short, he goes to Nature for his facts, not to somebody else's version of some one else's notion of what some one else thought the object might look like. In the one case, the American case, a man is supposed to be learning to draw. In the French case he is not learning to draw, because most Grand Prix men draw superlatively well before they win the Grand Prix—he is learning to be an architect, training his eye to recognize values of light and shade on an actual object; and all architecture is merely a matter of light and shade and all draughtsmanship is merely a means by which a man may learn how to distribute his light and shade in beautiful ways.

The best way for a man to learn to render details well is to study Nature for his facts, and to study the plates in *D'Espouy's Fragments d'Architecture* for his methods if he cannot come by some actual drawings by masters of the craft (as it is so difficult to do in this country). Direct photographs from the drawings are the next best thing to the drawings themselves.

Rendering at large scale varies from that at small scale, not in principle, but in details. The small scale imposes simplification. But all that has been "hereinbefore specified" applies to larger scale drawings. The suppression of line as line and its use merely as a guide for the edge of a wash, plane values, reflected lights and shadows, all these apply. But if we study Nature we will find things to give expression to and in the drawings in D'Espouy ways to express them.

I will not describe the making of a detail rendering because I should have to repeat much already said. Instead I shall point out some of the things you will or should observe in D'Espouy or in the illustrations in this book, and indicate how they are done.

One of the first things to know is that most of the detail drawings the Grand Prix men make are at quarter full size and that they gain considerably in effect of course in reduction for reproduction. They are nevertheless exquisitely done as a rule. But the execution of certain effects is much easier at large scale. At a large scale where the washes cover considerable area and where therefore defects have just so much more chance of occurring, it is all the more essential to success to build up the values slowly, pale wash by wash, and sponge off frequently—and this process of building up and sponging off is frequently carried on right through to the very end and a drawing with every value established and which looks to most eyes finished, is calmly sponged down and built up to value again and again until there is enough ink *in* the paper to require only one last fresh wash to give firmness and crispness. This is of course making drawings for the sake of making them—and only those who like to make drawings, as painters like to paint pictures, for the love and the fun of it, need apply.

The magical, unbelievable quality of such drawings can only be gotten by such methods. Needless to say they are in pure India Ink or practically so.

The detail shown in Plate No. 11 is at four feet to the inch but the gradation of the uppermost cyma was done as though the scale were much larger; a number of very light pencil lines were ruled parallel to the run of the molding and a series of

PLATE II

To illustrate the gradation of the shade on the cyma, and the shadow on the curved surface in the rake of the pediment, by a series of washes laid in bands. (See p. 96.) Also to show the narrow band of light left along the edge of the cornice shadow. (See p. 97.)

pale flat tones passed one after the other, covering first one band, then that one and the next above, then three, then four and so on until the darkest part has perhaps half a dozen washes and the lightest perhaps but one, and at a little distance the eye blends these bands (which are seen upon close inspection to be of distinctly different values) into one band with an even gradation. The same method was used as on the curved surface back of the chéneau on the rake of the pediment in the same drawing.

Light Edges. If you will look closely you will observe along the edge of a plane where it is relieved against another plane in Plate 14 and the edge of the obelisk in Plate No. 10, a light streak. This, so far as my observation goes, has only an occasional existence in Nature due to the weathering of stone under certain conditions, but is useful as a convention or dodge to give additional life and brilliancy to a drawing. It is of course prepared for in advance and the tone of this light edge is probably the original plane value established and which is left out in future washes in the process of piquage. (In fact, the whole process of rendering at large scale is little else but piquage.) The same is true of the narrow band of light you may frequently see on a frieze at the edge of the cornice shadow for instance. The cornice shadow is built up to value and then a wash is put on the lighted part of the frieze, very pale, leaving this narrow streak of the original tone of the frieze along the edge of the shadow. (This was done in Plate 11 which has lost something in reproduction.) The result is an immensely added brilliancy and softness. It would be perfectly possible to bring the frieze up to full value and then put the cornice shadow over it—but it would not be nearly so subtle nor nearly so brilliant and beautiful. Practically all the surfaces should be treated in this way;

first a general tone for the whole general plane, then the shadows built up, then the final plane value, leaving a narrow light along the edge of the shadow or the shade as the case may be. Planes in shadow may be treated in the same way but the light edges are reversed. But whether in light or in shadow it must not be obvious and at the proper focal distance, the distance at which all relations of forms and values may best be grasped, it should only be felt, not seen.

Penumbra. Sometimes, as in Plate No. 12, there is another convention adopted—the use of the penumbra. When the shadow of one object is cast upon another object by two differ- erent sources of light of the same intensity, such as two candles side by side, one shadow overlaps the other, the combined value of the two making up the mass of the shadow and that one of them which overlaps the other making a light shadowy edge which is the penumbra. So it is assumed that the sun has slipped a bit or has a brother and a penumbra appears along the edges of the shadows—usually only the important ones. The penumbra wash is put on last so as to wash down and soften the edge of the umbra or shadow, and is sometimes very narrow indeed, some- times quite wide. It has the effect of softening the edges of very dark shadows at a very large scale and keeping them from looking tinny and hard.

In Mr. Cret's drawing (Plate No. 13) of the details of his Valley Forge Memorial Arch it will be observed that he dis- cards the usual convention in his reflected lights and makes his shadows darker at their source nearest to the shadow-casting plane—in short, he assumed no plane below from which re- flected light would have been thrown back into his shadows. But he retains reflected shadows. All of which is entirely legitimate

TEMPLE DE MARS VENGEUR A ROME

PLATE 12   BY G. REDON

Reproduced from D'Espouy's Fragments d'Architecture Antique, Vol. I, Pl. 60

To illustrate the softening of the edge of a shadow in a large-scale drawing by the use of the penumbra, to avoid a hard and tinny appearance.   (See p. 98.)

and proper, I may say, for the benefit of those who need to be reassured as to the legitimacy and propriety of things.

Textures. Stippling and fine cross-hatching with the brush and with the pen are often resorted to to give texture and quality to surfaces. Here again the sponging off and building up process may be relied upon to produce exquisite subtleties of surface and of tone.

All sorts of things which one cannot show at a very small scale are possible at a larger scale and help to model and give brilliancy, such as the reflected light on the edges of window sash in shadow, as shown in Plate No. 8, a drawing at quarter scale. Such instances might be multiplied indefinitely but enough has been said to direct the attention of the student of rendering to points he might miss, and indicate how the trick is turned. With what he has been told in this volume he should be able to make a pretty close analysis of the methods employed and the steps followed in any drawing he examines, and such analysis by one's self is of more value than pages of disquisition and exposition.

VI

RENDERING PLANS

It is, I think, far more difficult to render plans well than elevations. We have Nature to guide us in the latter case and we may stand comfortably on the ground and make our observations. But the habit of flying is not yet sufficiently common to make the aspect of things from the sky familiar to many of us.[1] So that we have had to depend upon our imaginations. It is a perfectly safe generalization to say that the average Frenchman much excels the better-than-average American in rendering plans. Over and over again in the exhibitions at the Ecole des Beaux Arts one has a chance to compare the work of the two nationalities. It may even be compared to a degree in the *Medailles des Concours*, although the color and much of the handling is lost in reproduction. But there is a certain tightness, timidity, dryness amounting almost to primness, in the rendered plans and even the elevations of the freest moving American as compared with the French. I suppose it is the same temperamental quality which makes the American self-conscious in the *Rougevin* parades—too much Pilgrim Fathers. This tightness and dryness begins with the drawing, at the inking-in stage. The precision and exactitude, the fine line proper to elevations or sections are a positive detriment in the *entourage* of a plan. Broad, light, soft lines crossed freely at intersections

[1] Some of the aerial photographs, especially French ones, made from a point not very high from the ground are most suggestive as to treatment of masses of foliage, of shadows and the textures of open spaces.

PLATE 13   BY PAUL PHILIPE CRET

Illustrating, in this drawing of the details of Mr. Cret's
Valley Forge Memorial Arch, how the shadows are made
darker near the shadow-casting forms, but reflected
lights, shades and shadows are retained.   (See p. 98.)

with other lines are in order. The whole plan should look free and loose.

Cold and Warm Lines. It is not a bad idea to make a difference in the tone of the line you use for the interior of the building and for the outside entourage, cold inside and warm outside. A warm, brownish sort of line for floor or ceiling indication does not harmonize very well with the cold black of the *poché*.[1] The same criticism may be directed at warm washes in *demi-poché* (half-black value) or in pavements or the graded washes one puts on staircases to indicate "up" and "down"; when contrasted with the pure black of the walls they look muddy and dirty. They should, I think, always be cooled down with Blue.

Freedom of Workmanship. The plan of the building or buildings in a rendered plan is usually far too well drawn, too precise, too exact in appearance. To be sure, in competition drawings, we have to consider the dreaded Professional Adviser with his precious Computors who will nail you on cubage if they can, so one must actually be accurate. But that is why I used the expression "in appearance." They should be accurate without looking so. I can't tell you how this trick is turned except to say that you must keep your workmanship loose and free.

The whole question is, as usual, one of harmony of the *ensemble*. As in a rendered plan, the paths, roads, plantations of trees and shrubbery must be loose and free and avoid the tight and hard and dry, so also must the structure or structures have

[1] Poché is a French word (pronounced Po-shay) which indicates the darkened or blacked-in walls of a plan but which has also a sort of special significance meaning all the black of a plan. As: "Your *poché* is out of scale." "Your *poché* is thin." "The *poché* is fine but the *entourage* is not well studied. And since "blacked-in walls" is a clumsier expression than "poché" I shall use the latter.

a free quality. This is of the first importance in plans at a small scale where the entourage predominates, where it is the general scheme which counts and not the precise arrangement of any detail. I remember in this connection years ago in Paris, a plan submitted by Tony Garnier, son of Charles, in a competition for one of the special prizes offered at the Ecole, the subject being one in which the treatment of the landscape was of paramount importance. There was something about Garnier's poché which differed from the others. It had more sparkle, more strength, more value. Examined closely it was a mess of black blobs put in apparently at top speed, carelessly, freehand. But one of the men in the same âtelier with Garnier told me that he carefully inked in that poché with a quill pen tied to the end of a long stick and that he put the plan on the ground, got up on a stool *and made the poché look right from a distance.*

The plan of a building in a city, without entourage and un-rendered, may of course be very beautifully and precisely drawn, but the moment you surround it with planting or even with grass plots, beware!

Pattern. Plan is after all, aside from the virtues of arrange-ment, of circulation, of convenience, of economy without mean-ness, pretty nearly pure pattern—much more so than elevation in which the third dimension destroys so many fond hopes of a design conceived as a pattern in only two. I would not be under-stood as claiming that a plan should not have a sense of the third dimension. *That* is a question of design. I am assuming that we are to render a good design. And when we render a plan it is to bring out the beauty of the pattern in it. Everything must contribute to that beauty—the weight of the poché, that is to say the thickness of the walls of the structures, the widths and color of the circulatory system inside and outside the building, the value of the grass and trees and shrubs and their shadows (or the absence of shadows), the big relations of the big lights and darks, the emphasis to place on this or the other element of the plan to bring out the shapes we want to define, the suppression or subordination of unpleasant shapes.

Treatment in Relation to Scale. As in elevations, the scale of a drawing should establish the character of the rendering of a plan. We must adopt a breadth of treatment in direct relation to the scale. The smaller it is the more we must avoid meticulous detail. Trees in which at a large scale we would permit ourselves a certain amount of modeling become merely dark masses relieved from complete flatness only by the settling out of the pigments.

These general considerations being disposed of we may take up processes more in detail.

Penciling In. The penciling process is precisely similar to that for an elevation.

Inking in a Plan. In inking in, if we decide to make our light lines inside the plan cold and our entourage lines warm we will have three inks to deal with, because the poché must be outlined in pure black ink. For this Higgins's Waterproof Ink is satisfactory. In doing so you have before you two alternatives —to use a very fine line, almost a hair line, which you cross crisply but not exaggeratedly at all intersections, and a much coarser line crossed in the same way. In any small scale plan, sixty-fourth and thirty-second scale, and sometimes even at sixteenth scale, the fine line is the better except that it makes for great precision and exactitude of appearance. At window and door openings I like to see the lines of the jambs prolonged a bit inside and outside of the wall and the lines of the inner and outer wall faces *almost* stopped against them; that is, with very little run-over. The same with openings in interior walls. The plan reads more clearly. The lines representing the frames and sash of windows should be inked in with a very fine line with light ink, so that the window opening will not be clogged up with heavy dark lines. Here is one of those many chances we have in draughtsmanship for the exercise of common sense in indication—the window being for the purpose of lighting the interior it ought to look as though the light could go through easily.

Poché. Although outlining the poché preliminary to blacking in the walls is not necessarily the next process, it may be if you like. This means running a broad black line inside of the real outline. It may be omitted by any one with the courage to pocher the walls without it, but I believe it saves time and profanity. This also may be done with Higgins's ink, but the line must not be so wide as to show as a broad dull edge around every piece of poché—for plain Higgins's ink dries dull and our poché is to be a brilliant, glossy black which we obtain by putting Higgins's ink in our slate grinding-saucer and grinding India Ink in it until it is so thick that when we blow it gently back from the edge of the saucer it flows back quite slowly; until it does this it is not thick enough. I have found good thick India Ink poché mixed like this entirely satisfactory. Some very particular persons put sugar in it to make it shine more. This poché is put in the walls with a very fine brush, or with a ruling pen provided the surface of the paper is not scraped, which of course makes a dull furry place at once.

For those who like dead black poché Mr. Goodhue tells me

PLATE 14   BY G. ANCELET

Reproduced from D'Espouy's Fragments d'Architecture Antique, Vol. I, Pl. 33

To illustrate the convention of a light band along the edge of a form to help relieve it against another plane or to make forms read clearly in a shadow (as in that of the pedestal and vase). This device is used in many places in this drawing. It will repay the closest possible study. (See p. 97.)

that his plan for the Nebraska State Capitol was poché with Peach Black and Prussian Blue over India Ink which produced a deep rich black perfectly dead.

A good many men defer the pocher-ing of the plan until after it is all rendered, so that the glossiness of the poché may not be injured by the friction of T-square and triangle. This seeems to me a grave mistake. I fail to see how any value whether of wash or line can be judged unless the masses of black poché are established. They constitute a value of overwhelming strength which must be worked up to. Half the disappointments we have in rendered plans are due to bad guesses made without the poché to guide us. This is true not merely of washes but of the values of lines in floor and ceiling indications and of entourage. It seems more sensible to go over the poché again where it has been dulled than to run the risk of a large general failure.

Floor and Ceiling Indication. We may consider floor and ceiling indication as the next step. The first important decision to make is whether we will leave the circulation white and make the rooms grey or vice versa. Either one it must be. A plan left with too little grey in it looks meager, empty and blank; and one which is grey all over errs at the opposite extreme, looks surcharged and stupid and is very hard to read. There are many plans of such a character that they look best with the circulation grey and the rooms white.

Furniture. It is the custom of some men to furnish the rooms with indications of chairs and tables besides lines indicating floor borders. This is difficult to do well but if well and intelligently done helps to express the meaning of the plan; for example, an oblong table in the middle of a room with chairs around it is the usual indication for a Committee Room and hardly needs the printed words to designate it as such—and a semi-circular row of seats with a long table at the center with a couple of other tables near by indicates to the initiated eye a Grand Jury Room. Court Rooms are furnished according to the character of the business done in them; Courts of Appeal, naturally, have no jury therefore no jury box. And so on.

If you elect to furnish the rooms it will grey them to such an extent that the circulation must be white. The furniture indication should be so managed in relation to the floor indication that the spaces enclosed by the outlines of the furniture sparkle if they are to be left white. No space large or small will sparkle if enclosed with a thin line and these furniture and floor lines should be broad, soft looking lines. But sometimes a light wash is put on every piece of furniture, substituting another value for white.

The first step toward "furnishing" the plan (an expression used to express its dressing-up with or without tables and chairs) is to run a line very close to the poché to soften the sharp contrast between its black and the white of the plan. And here if anywhere a line is apt to look wiry. It should be a good fat line even at a very small scale such as thirty-two feet to the inch. This line is like a base line and should stop at all doorways and at all windows opening to the floor. The fine line you have used to outline your poché and which I said should be prolonged somewhat at the jambs of openings will be found very useful to stop this base line against. Another point as to width of line is worth mentioning—that the fewer lines you use to furnish your plan the wider and softer they should be. Oftentimes there is no time for very elaborate indications and one wide line has to do duty for two thinner ones.

Expression of Character. The arrangement of the other lines is, of course, a matter of design, of pattern, and of judgment and taste. The treatment appropriate to a Public Library is not one suitable to a simple schoolhouse. Besides this distinction in general character, that between the characters of different rooms in the same building is to be made. While one might be prepared to find elaborate ceiling or floor patterns in a drawing room it would be somewhat surprising to find them in the kitchen. There are two goals, both of which must be reached for a real success; first, to make all parts of your furnishing contribute to the general pattern of your plan, make it count as you want it to count as a whole; second, to make the details appropriate in their own characters. If the kitchen needs a good deal of grey to avoid a light spot which would disturb the ensemble, get it by such simple and appropriate indication as a tiled floor, not by a Ducal Palace ceiling. The Grand Prix *projets* should be carefully studied for all this sort of thing, especially those prior to about 1890 before the taste of the school became too much vitiated and plan became pattern to such an extent that it ceased to be plan. *Letarouilly's Edifices de Rome Moderne* is valuable for reference for both ceiling and floor indications.

Washes may frequently be used to produce greys, sometimes so faint that they can hardly be perceived close by. But any modification of pure white however slight has its effect. One may run a wash in the border around a room or over the field and if there is furniture it may be left white or rendered as you please.

Indoor and Outdoor Scale. The relative scale of indoor

and outdoor patterns such as pavements should also be compared and studied. Observe that the outdoor scale is always larger and simpler in the best examples and that some of the patterns which are the richest in appearance are produced with great economy of means. The lines used for entourage must be good fat lines, soft and light in the main, strengthened where accent or stiffening up is necessary. They should be made quite a bit darker at the beginning than you want them ultimately to be, to allow for sponging down or rubbing down—for in rendering a plan, if you pocher before putting in your greys you will have to clean off with a rubber or art gum instead of sponging off.

Let us mark here a strong difference between plan and elevation. The delicacies and subtleties of handling one observes in rendering an elevation are largely lost in rendering a plan. The paper must be kept clean of course and it must not be greasy, but the same degree of care need not be taken to preserve every inch of surface in perfect condition.

Study of Tree Masses and Entourage Generally. Before the lines of the entourage (what the French sometimes call *sauce*) are inked in, the tree and shrubbery plantations should be studied carefully so that where their masses overhang paths and other elements of the plan you may stop the lines against them instead of running them through. Of course, all such breaks in the continuity of the formal lines must be carefully studied with reference to their effect upon the general pattern and composition—and it is to insure their proper effect that I recommend their careful study rather than leaving them to improvisation later on and consequent regrets. The outlines of the foliage should not be inked in as a rule. They are better if left in very light pencil. The outlines of hedges I recommend inking in free hand with an irregular wiggly line, pretty dark because the hedges will be rendered dark.

Conventional Indications. The beginner is recommended to study carefully all the good plans he can have access to and learn the significance of the various indications. The French, for instance, to indicate trees planted each side of a road use dots for the tree trunks, usually with their shadows sharply graded, and the dots connected either with lines straight across the road from dot to dot, or with diagonal lines forming a criss-cross pattern. They do not show these trees with all their foliage in plan as though looking down on top of them, for this would destroy the width of the road which in pattern counts as a light broad band and which they wish to preserve. But in all these matters it is what you wish to bring out, how you want the elements of your plan to count, which govern.

As I have said, one of the defects to guard against is a meager, thin, flat, tinny appearance. The usual cause of this is the use of too few lines and bands especially along the edges of greenswards, flower beds or plantations. Of course, you will have studied the black and white and grey masses of your plan thoroughly, perhaps in soft pencil before you begin to render, and have a very clear idea of what you want to do. You will find when you come to translate these rough studies into a serious drawing most of the go and spirit of the sketch have evaporated. When your plan is studied and inked in and ready to render *it should look much too rich;* a plan simplifies so when rendered that you need a multiplicity of lines and bands as edges for your masses. *Never,* for instance, use a single line, however broad and soft you make it, on the edge of a grass plot. Whether a curb would be there in execution or not, the line must be doubled to avoid making the mass of greensward look like tin. And frequently and usually a band of a darker or lighter color near the edge is needed, the band itself defined each side with a double line. In execution you may not want or be able to afford the curbs or ivy borders or hedges or whatever these bands and lines and borders are supposed to represent, but you need them in the drawing if you want to avoid the dryness and lack of sparkle and interest of all too many plans.

Washes. As for the actual application of the washes, the same general principles apply as in elevations—your lightest tones go on first. But it is not necessary to build up your tones so gradually. When rendering a plan in monotone (perhaps in a competition where color is barred) a combination of India Ink and Peach Black is excellent, both of them toned of course; the tones which will ultimately stand for roads, paths, pavements and the like may be built up nearly to value with India Ink, which has no texture, and then a thin wash with Peach Black as a base floated over, which will give texture and yet be fresh and transparent in appearance—for it must be remembered that heavy washes of Peach Black or Charcoal Grey look carbonaceous and hard at the edges. Be sure to have a good water-table line around your building or buildings to stop the washes against. This is not inconsistent with my former remarks about these lines —I'm talking about plans now, not elevations, and if your wash doesn't exactly touch the line everywhere, or consume it, or if it runs over it here and there, it makes for the freer, looser effect we look for in a plan. But in saying this I have not issued a license to be sloppy—merely to be carefully careless.

Gradation. Before we have floated any wash, we have of course as previously remarked, made rough studies to determine the general appearance of the plan. There are cases in which it should grade from dark at the top to light at the bottom, others from dark at the bottom to light at the top and others in which the light and dark may be concentrated around some element of the plan we specially want to emphasize—the law of contrast at work again. Decide what you intend to do, be sure you're right and stick to your scheme.

In working up from light to dark as usual, roads and paths will be the lightest, the grass next, certain bands darker, others lighter, than the grass, trees darker than the grass and the shadows darkest of all except the hedges or the bands we want for accent. In all grass or foliage tones and shadows it is advisable to use a great deal of deposing pigment, when we are working in color. All tones should be sharply graded. For example, besides the general gradation of the plan, each grass plot should be graded in itself (by grass plot I mean any separate grassy area). Bands and hedges and borders should be very sharply graded indeed. For trees and shrubbery or tree masses it is well to tilt the board sharply and diagonally—that is to say in such a manner that the wash will run toward the lower right hand side of the forms and settle there. This gives, without the labor of grading out, and far better, a light and a dark side to your trees.

Trees in Perspective. There is another convention sometimes adopted and which is very effective (Plate No. 15)—drawing certain trees such as cedars, poplars, or any trees or groups which are to be emphasized or used as accents, in perspective, so that the plan presents an appearance somewhere between a plan and a bird's-eye view. This is particularly effective for the planting in interior courts. It takes a great deal of skill and has to be done with a sure hand. No one who has not drawn tree forms from Nature should attempt it.

Sponging-in Tree Forms. Another way to indicate tree forms is to tear off a piece from a rather coarse sponge, soak it thoroughly, first in water which you squeeze out, and then in your wash (of which you need a lot for this method) and put on the tree forms with it. As you touch the paper you squeeze the sponge a little so that the wash will run out of it. The position of the sponge should be constantly changed to bring different parts of the torn filaments in contact with the paper and so vary the forms you are producing. This is a very good way when in a hurry, but it is rather difficult to control. Well done it is full of delightful accidental effects. For a drawing where the tree masses have been as carefully studied as a landscape architect would arrange them, the brush is the thing to use.

Shadows. The treatment of the shadows depends like everything else upon the scale of the drawing. In a large drawing we frequently load a large brush and put on the shadows with the *side* of it. This also, like so many things, must be skilfully done. As a general thing the point of the brush should be used. The trees and tree masses should have little shadows put in very wet with a crisp firm touch and *left alone,* not messed with and made muddy. Make them dark enough to start with. The tyro is usually timid and makes these accents too pale; they dry out too light and he goes on puddling and patting and stabbing in the blind hope that some miracle will make them come right.

Fountains, flagpoles, rostral columns and like elements very often have their shadows cast, very swiftly graded. In a garden it frequently explains the treatment if the shadows of hedges,

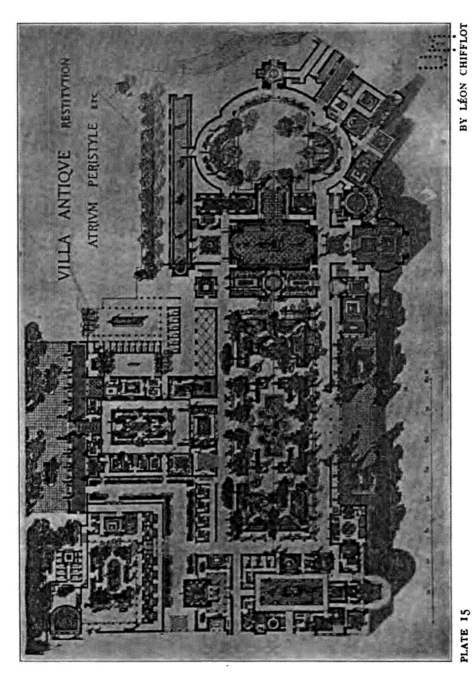

VILLA ANTIQVE RESTITVTION

ATRIVM PERISTYLE ETC

BY LÉON CHIFFLOT

PLATE 15

Reproduced from D'Espouy's Fragments d'Architecture Antique, Vol. II, Pl. 70

Illustrating the use of trees, fountains, statues and hedges in perspective, with their shadows, in an otherwise geometrical plan. (See p. III.)

vases, clipped trees, pedestals, all the shadow-casting forms, are carefully drawn and rendered. When carefully and thoughtfully done, the entire character of the design is so completely revealed that no section or elevation is needed to explain it. Although I indicated above that the shadows are the darkest value except hedges and so on, I was referring to monotone rendering. This must not be taken as an absolute rule nor as applying to rendering in color. I have seen a very beautiful rendering of a garden in which the shadows were yellow and gave a charming effect of sunlight.

Cloud Shadows. Sometimes when a part of a plan is perforce uninteresting it may be given quality and interest by floating a big cloud shadow over it, breaking the shadow up so as to dapple the area with sunlight and shadow.

Air Brush. The atomizer or the air-brush may be used to great advantage in a plan. Streets which run out of the picture always chop the plan up into sections and the effect of these bands, leading the eye out right and left and top and bottom, is to contradict and nullify that effect of concentration of interest which is essential. Therefore they should be darkened toward the edges of the plan, which will correct the effect of diffusion of interest and unite the blocks of buildings or properties into one mass instead of a series of dislocated spots. The atomizer is very good for this and will do the trick in a tenth the time required with the brush. It is good too for uniting the tree masses and to put on a unifying tone when the drawing has gotten spotty or out of key. It will give texture in an India Ink drawing. It is very useful but it must not be abused.

Block Plans. There are a few wrinkles about block plans which it may be useful to communicate. The usual way to present a block plan is to make the buildings dark, but they look very well if left white—the whole plan sparkles. If they are to be dark, try inking in the silhouette of the building with a jet black strong line and draw a fine grey line all around inside, leaving a narrow band of white between. The fine grey line is the guide line for the dark wash. The band of white between the wash and the black silhouette gives life and brilliancy. When the wash comes up to the silhouette it looks dull and stodgy by comparison. A similar treatment may be given blocks of buildings, the silhouette not necessarily in a black line, but the principle of a light band between silhouette and wash being maintained.

It also gives scale and interest to draw the reveals of all door and window openings (back to the frame or glass line) and all recessed portions, as well, of course, as columns and pilasters, even at so small a scale as sixty-four feet to the inch, instead of drawing a mere straight line for the silhouette of the building. It not merely has more interest, but when paths or roads lead up to entrances, their reason is made apparent and the relation between building and grounds is made clearer.

Temperament. There are doubtless some who will say that in all this matter of academic rendering no allowance is made for temperament and that in reducing things to an orderly method we become cold, lifeless and inartistic. This I believe to be at once the point of view and the defense-in-advance of the lazy, the heedless and the impatient, and such people are always looking for short cuts. They do not write "Perfection or Bust!" on the inside of their heads so they can see it every time they close their eyes. There is an awful lot of twaddle current about temperament. If a man is slovenly in work or person he claims it as an expression of his "temperament." If he is self-indulgent and won't buckle down to a hard day's work he is too temperamental to be confined. If he is muddle-headed, or illogical and unable to follow out a course of reasoning, temperament is the cause. And because temperament is rated as something worth having, these "temperamental" weaknesses and defects are erected into virtues. Temperament *is* worth having—under control. But fear not! The real thing will show in your work, no matter how systematic and orderly you are about your methods. Order and method are the very handmaidens of temperament—they do her chores for her and leave her spirit free.

Do you suppose Jules Guérin and Maxfield Parrish could do the things they do without method? To the expert eye method sticks out all over their work—careful planning 'way ahead for the effect that charms us so—a vision seen and held through a dozen processes and stages. These men are both magnificent craftmen. They know their job. One of them I know is an orderly workman and I'd wager anything you like the other is. And you don't hear men of their stamp talking about temperament.

And finally, as to rendering, a fine rendering is like a well dressed man or woman. The vulgar person, like the vulgar drawing, is bedizened in the hope of attracting attention—and they both do, but not the kind of attention worth having. Make your drawing look like a good deed in a naughty world.

VII

THE PROPERTIES OF PIGMENTS

Water Color Pigments. Winsor and Newton's pigments are the Anglo-Saxon standard. Excellent and pure pigments are also made by Hatfield of Boston. I like them best in tubes or half tubes, because they keep soft for a long time, and the harder pan colors wear out a favorite carefully chosen brush. Suit yourself. If you elect for pans you will be in company no less distinguished than that of Jules Guérin. But don't use your best brush to mix your colors with in that case—use an old one.

Light and Heavy Pigments. In the interest of simplicity these pigments may be grouped into two classes irrespective of their color—as transparent or light weight, and as opaque, heavy, or "deposing" (from the French *déposer*, to deposit). And this classification is of particular value to the renderer.

	Transparent or Light-Weight Pigments	*Opaque, Heavy and Deposing Pigments*
Reds	Carmine	Vermilion
	Alizarin Crimson	Light Red
	Rose Madder	Burnt Sienna
Yellows	Gamboge	Raw Sienna
	Gall Stone or Ox Gall	Cadmium Pale
		Yellow Ochre
Green	....	Viridian (Verte Emeraude)

	Transparent or Light-Weight Pigments	*Opaque, Heavy and Deposing Pigments*
Blues	Prussian Blue	Cobalt
		French or Ultramarine
		Smalt
Grey	Payne's Grey (Bluish)	
Blacks	. . . .	Charcoal Grey
		Peach Black
		Ivory Black

There is, of course, but one good way to learn the characteristics of these colors and that is to try them out in mixtures. It will do no harm, however, to indicate what may be expected. First as to their individual properties:

Properties of Pigments.

Carmine: A beautiful, transparent crimson red of great strength. A very little goes a great way.

Alizarin Crimson: Very like Carmine but somewhat sharper and harsher to the trained eye. It is an aniline color and used to be rated as fugitive. Some chemists say that aniline colors as now made are permanent. The best way is to try them out. Lay a flat wash of Carmine side by side with one of Alizarin Crimson, cut the paper in half, put one half away in a drawer out of the light and pin the other up in a good bright light. Compare them at the end of a month and form your judgment on the result. If you really want to know about colors, do the same with all of them, pure and in mixtures. You'll learn more about their durability in a month in this than in any other way.

Rose Madder: A beautiful rose-colored transparent pigment of very little strength in mixtures. It used to be rated as very fugitive. Greater permanency is claimed for it now if the drawing is afterwards protected against damp air by glass. A valid objection to its use in water color lies in the fact that it is made of the madder root and deposits in a thin film or scum, on the paper, which lifts and stirs if the wash is worked over or through again as is so frequently necessary, and makes the wash look muddy and messy.

Vermilion (English): A brilliant Red inclining toward Yellow rather than Blue, of great weight, which settles or deposes very swiftly. A wash in which Vermilion occurs must be kept moving and not allowed to stand for an instant or streaks or areas of red will appear. This is all very well and highly desirable in free water color work, particularly if you control the settling process—of which, later on.

Light Red: This is classed among the heavy colors because it is so opaque, although it does not settle out very much. But it is very powerful, and a very little bit will strongly affect a big wash. Its usefulness lies in its faculty for helping make Greys. Cobalt Blue with a mere touch of Light Red makes a beautiful transparent Grey. A little more Red and you have a Violet of low value.

Burnt Sienna: This is classed among the Reds because it belongs rather with them than with the Yellows. It is very heavy and settles out beautifully in a wash of just the right wetness. In combination with French or Ultramarine Blue, with a very slight admixture of Carmine, I have rendered a great many elevations and plans as well. By varying the speed at which you move the wash you may make such a mixture settle out to a great variety of tones. The French Blue being heavier than the Burnt Sienna, it settles a bit faster. Therefore, if you pull the wash fast and don't give the Blue time to settle out, the Burnt Sienna has a chance and the wash dries out warmer. If you pull it slowly and give the Blue a chance to settle, the Blue will predominate when dry. The Carmine being light and transparent is not affected by the speed of the brush; it is added as a corrective of a tendency there is, when the Blue and Sienna are in certain proportions, to make a greenish tone.

Gamboge: A beautiful, transparent Yellow slightly inclined toward greenish. It combines well with French Blue, Carmine, Vermilion, Cadmium and Viridian. In naturalistic and free rendering it is invaluable for the greens of foliage and of grass. With the admixture of a little Vermilion in places and of Viridian in others it is fine for the representation of gold mosaics and the like. It is not for use in formal rendering with India Ink.

Aureolin Yellow: Also slightly inclined toward greenish but most useful, powerful and beautiful.

Gall-Stone or Ox-Gall: This is one of the most seductive and deceptive of pigments. Mixed with black it gives a wonderful transparency, warmth and depth to the shadows—for about a week. Then it has all faded and the charm and character the drawing showed is exchanged for a lifeless greenish hue. It should be rigorously excluded from the working palette, as all fugitive colors should be.

Raw Sienna: This pigment is the same earth as Burnt Sienna but the latter is roasted; they therefore look nothing alike, but have the same weight and depose at the same rate. Raw Sienna may be used in formal rendering with India Ink as a base. It is quite a light yellow when diluted and with the black of the ink, of course produces a greenish tone which has to be corrected by

Carmine. The effect of a rendering in which it is used as the principal toning agent is rather cold. But it gives a very stony look to stone when used for local color and the cold effect may be counterbalanced by warming up the shadows with Burnt Sienna.

Cadmium Pale: An opaque golden yellow, little if any used in formal rendering, but excellent in free water color work. It has body, and combines with Gamboge to make a third beautiful yellow. It does not noticeably depose.

Yellow Ochre: Like Cadmium, Yellow Ochre does not depose, but it is an earth and not transparent. Ingres called it, in oils, a "heaven-sent pigment." It is useful in some ways and at certain times in free rendering. But I should banish it from the formal rendering palette. It has been a kind of superstition handed down in the schools that if you want to get sunlight and warmth into a drawing, float a wash of Yellow Ochre over the paper first. Or, if you have finished a water color and have failed to get sunlight and warmth in it, float a wash of Yellow Ochre over it. Permit me to say that these recipes are entirely fallacious except for a body color drawing and that either process is guaranteed to take the life out of a drawing in transparent color in the shortest possible time. It is peculiarly deadly over a completed drawing, for the opaque particles of the earth form a film or scum over everything. The first thing it does to white paper is to kill its reflecting power—and it is the white paper throwing the light back to the eye through the washes which gives the drawing transparency, depth, and brilliancy. Jules Guérin includes it in his regular working palette. (See page 129). But he knows how and where and when to use it; he works not only in very close values but principally in body color—harmonies rather than contrasts—diffused light rather than sunlight.

PLATE 16

BY FRANK HAZELL

The cast shadows of the buildings around the court are admirably utilized in the composition. The drawing is an opaque water-color on a slightly rough grey paper. The grey shadows in the foreground and on the building were first tinted with thin, almost transparent, washes of blue, purple, red and yellow in different places on the wet paper, allowing the colors to blend but retaining the value of the shadows. This gives it a luminous quality and accentuates the sunlight. The general color scheme is simple. A wash of orange over the grey paper gives the effect of the mellow tiles of the roof. The walls and the stone flagging are done in Chinese White toned with yellow and orange.

Frank Hazell, who paints sunlight as few men can, floats it over the paper first; but he too works chiefly in body color wherein the Chinese White takes the place of the white paper. He says he gets immense brilliancy by allowing the Yellow Ochre, sometimes quite deep and strong, to show as the high lights. So I repeat it has its place and its great value, but not in formal rendering.

Viridian: This is the equivalent in water color of Verte Emeraude in oils and which latter is not at all the same as Emerald Green although this would be a literal translation. Viridian and Verte Emeraude are both made from Oxide of Chromium and are pure and permanent pigments. Emerald Green is made from copper and in certain mixtures will destroy other colors by chemical action. Viridian is neither so powerful nor so heavy as Emerald Green but is a deposing color nevertheless. In formal rendering in color it is good for giving the effect of copper roofs, bronze doors and the like. In free rendering, for foliage and shutters and so on. And for certain skies, invaluable. Cobalt with some Viridian makes a marvelous blue sky.

Cobalt: Perhaps the most beautiful and useful of all the Blues. It is as near pure *blue* as pigments come, inclining neither to greenish nor purplish. It is not powerful, but it settles or deposes beautifully. It is good for almost every use. In formal rendering, a touch of it in India Ink gives a sky with air in it, or bathes a distant plane in atmosphere.

French or Ultramarine Blue: ("New Blue" is very similar —said not to be as pure or permanent.) A rich and splendid blue—what might be called a "warm" blue, inclining more toward purplish than Cobalt does. It is very heavy and settles out well in all mixtures. The writer uses it a great deal both in free water colors and in formal rendering. But it is too heavy for distant planes or skies in formal rendering or for skies in free work.

Ultramarine and Vermilion form a mutually destructive mixture and turn each other black by chemical action.

Prussian Blue: A greenish blue. The only use I have been able to find for this pigment is in free rendering in certain aspects of moonlight to give a strong greenish cast without using heavy color which would settle too much for the special effect to be rendered.

Smalt: Smalt is very little used. It is the heaviest color of which I know, made of ground blue glass which settles instantly, and has to be manipulated at lightning speed and very wet and with the greatest skill. The particles of color lift and shift when another wash is passed over it and the result is apt to be muddy. It is usually used the last thing as a floated wash to make the drawing look as though it were done all at once, swiftly, and wet.

Payne's Grey: This color Jules Guérin includes in his permanent working palette as an equivalent for black, useful for certain greys or to make a bluish black. It is dangerous to have on the palette as a regular thing and should only be squeezed out when needed, because the brush may only too easily wander to it and it chills off some colors, makes others muddy and greys all down (reduces their "value"). Like Rose Madder or Brown Madder, it is deposited like a kind of scum on the paper which lifts when the wash is gone over again. It must be remembered however, that the way a thing is done makes all the difference in the world.

Charcoal Grey and *Peach Black:* The first is a rather cold, the second a rather warm black. They both have their advocates, and their friends sometimes advise their use as substitutes for India Ink in formal rendering, because they settle and give a certain amount of texture to a wash, especially in cases where there is not much time to work up a texture. But having tried them thoroughly and been thoroughly tried by them, I use them no more except as a pale final wash for the sake of texture. Washes of these pigments are carbonaceous in quality. The particles of color are very light (Charcoal Grey is made from charcoal) and float off to the edges of a wet wash and deposit themselves in a sooty little line. Also a wash of these pigments won't bear much working over as is necessary in building up a value in strong shadows.

Ivory Black: A warm black which, to me, for formal rendering, partakes of the defects of Peach Black and Charcoal Grey. There is no black like strained India Ink. It produces no effect of texture, but there are ways of overcoming that, beautifully and easily.

Be sure, before beginning work with these or any pigments, to examine them to see that they are in good condition. Old dry colors will sometimes fail to dissolve or unite with other colors or the India Ink.

Pace in Running Washes. It must be firmly borne in mind that the proportion of one pigment to another in a wash produces totally different results at slow or fast speed. I remember on one occasion, working with a man who used exactly the same palette of colors as I do, I mixed up a tone for the copper roofs on his elevation and mine—to be a greenish grey like weathered copper. I mixed, of course, with reference to my own pace and personal technique and I knew just what was in it. When my roof had dried out it was just what I expected it to be. His was nothing like mine nor like weathered copper. I was no more skilful than he. The result would have been reversed had he mixed the wash. He would instinctively have mixed it with reference to his own methods of handling, speed in manipulation and so on. There was a good deal of Emerald Green in the wash. I pulled it fast and not too wet so that the heavy particles of the Emerald Green would not have a chance to deposit unevenly or too much. He probably worked slowly and pretty wet.

I relate this incident because I learned so much from it. And I date a more complete and accurate knowledge of the properties of water colors and their manipulation from it because it set me thinking. Among the things it taught me is the secret of regulating the speed of washes according to their composition. Until one's knowledge of pigments and how they will act is accurate—quasi-scientific if you like—one is not master of his materials. They must be under his control. Particularly in free water color rendering by a real master of his craft, much that looks like happy accident is deliberately planned to happen.

In Nature the infinite variety of tones we see are produced by the effect of the red, green and violet rays of the spectrum on the nervous structure of the retina. To represent these tones in Nature by the use of pigments, however, we must use the three so-called primary colors—red, yellow, and blue. With combinations of the different reds, yellows and blues described above any gamut of tones may be established to suit the taste and temperament of the painter. The best way to find out what they will do in mixtures is to try them out, laying a series of small graded washes, running them fast and running them slow and noting the combination and speed beside each. But in the meantime this is what they do in combination:

> Red and Blue make Violet (Purple);
> Red and Yellow make Orange.
> Yellow and Blue make Green.

To make Grey—Take Red and Blue and mix a Violet. Add Yellow to it until the desired Grey is reached. Make it darker or lighter by the proportion of pigment to the water.

To make Brown—Take Red and Yellow and mix an Orange. Add Blue to it until you get the Brown you want, darker or lighter according to the proportions of pigment and water.

Observe that in making Grey and Brown you use exactly the same colors; the difference in the proportion of each makes Grey or Brown. The reason for mixing a Violet first as a basis for Grey and for mixing Orange as a basis for Brown is simple and obvious.—If you mix Yellow and Blue, which makes a Green and add Red to it until you get the Grey you want you'll do quite a bit of mixing and adding before you get it. Violet is simply nearer to a Grey than Green. The same principle applies in making Brown—Orange, a combination of Red and Yellow is nearer to Brown than either Violet or Green and therefore simpler and easier and surer to start out with.

You now have, with three simple colors as a starting point, a total of eight colors—Red, Yellow, Blue, Violet, Orange, Green, Grey and Brown. And you have the possibility of all the tones there are by varying the proportion of each constitutent. By an increase of Red over Blue in Violet you get a reddish or warmer Violet which is Purple; more Blue than Red gives a colder, because bluer, Violet. (Colors are rated as warmer or colder as they incline to the Red or the Violet end of the spectrum—in which the gradation is as follows from left to right: Red—Orange—Yellow—Green—Blue—Violet.   The transitional colors are here omitted.)   It is thus possible to mix, with Red, Blue and Yellow, a warm or reddish Grey, a bluish Grey or a yellowish Grey, far more subtle in quality than a ready mixed Grey and having by its make-up a definite affinity with all the other tones you use because it is made from the same basic pigments.   The same is true of Brown or Green.   With the exception of Viridian I avoid all ready mixed greens.   Blue and Yellow give, I think, much more beautiful Greens inclining to Blue or Yellow as the case demands.   For certain Greens just Viridian and Yellow will do it.

Working Palette.   It is important in establishing a working palette of pigments (I use the word "pigments" deliberately here instead of "colors") to make it as simple as possible, with as few colors as possible, and to choose such pigments as combine well together and give clear, pure tones, not muddy ones.   For instance, Carmine and Cobalt, Carmine and French Blue, or Cobalt and Vermilion make beautiful clear, pure Violets.   Prussian Blue and Carmine or Prussian Blue and Crimson Lake produce just mud.   It is well to have more than one Red, Yellow and Blue in your palette because each pigment of these colors has different qualities.

This is the writer's working palette:

Vermilion—a heavy Red inclining to Yellow.
Carmine—a transparent, crimson Red inclining to Violet rather than Yellow.

Cadmium Pale—an opaque golden Yellow.

Gamboge—a transparent Yellow inclining to Green.

Viridian—a heavy Green of cold tone.

Cobalt Blue—a heavy *pure* Blue.

French (or Ultramarine) Blue—a heavier Blue inclining toward Violet.

To these for special purposes on special occasions and for formal rendering are added:

Burnt Sienna—for both formal and free rendering.

Light Red—very occasionally for Greys with Cobalt and certain dull tones of Red.

Raw Sienna—for formal rendering occasionally.

Yellow Ochre—in free rendering occasionally in Greys or earth tones.

Payne's Grey—in free rendering to deepen Violets or Blues or take the place of Black.

Chinese (Zinc) White—Useful on occasions in both free and formal rendering—in the latter to retrieve blunders but never otherwise except in rapid work where it would take too long to leave out brilliant high lights.

All of the seven pigments first given combine perfectly. Of course, one may make mud with them as with any palette, but their weights and consistencies go together admirably. Chemically, French Blue and Vermilion in mixture are bad and go black in time. Cobalt and Vermilion are safe. The addition of Chinese White, which is opaque and made of zinc, to any other pigment makes an opaque mixture. White is added to other pigments in oil color painting to lighten them, but in water color painting the white is supplied by the white of the paper and, as before stated, it is the white surface throwing back the light through the film of color particles deposited on it in the wash which gives brilliancy and freshness to the drawing. This is a good thing to remember in working on colored paper and is, of course, the reason why, in order to get brilliancy in such drawings, the white lacking in the paper is frequently supplied by the use of Chinese White either throughout or in places. A painting in which Chinese White is used throughout is said to be made in "body color"; *"gouache"* is another term for it, though gouache colors strictly speaking come ready prepared with the zinc white mixed in them.

A point so obvious that it doesn't occur readily to one is this: If we color two equal areas (say a quarter of an inch square) with the same wash exactly, using quite a dry brush in the one case and a loaded one in the other, *the latter is darker,* for there are more particles of pigment suspended in the larger amount of water placed in the same area and when the water evaporates they are left behind. Color is prepared from various earths and chemicals, vegetable and animal substances in the form of powder, to which, for water colors, water and glycerine are added, oil for oil colors, glue and water for distemper, egg and vinegar for Tempera, the powder being practically the same for all; in Water Color it may be clearly and easily demonstrated that the color is produced on the paper by the deposit of the tiny, sometimes almost microscopic, particles of powder; thus, in a Violet wash, Red and Blue particles are deposited side by side and produce the effect of Violet on the eye; the thinner the wash we lay (that is, the more water in proportion to the pigment) the fewer the particles of powder on the paper and therefore the paler the Violet, or Red, or Blue, or any other color.

Jules Guérin's working palette is as follows: It is applicable only to free rendering, for this great artist does not, now at any rate, make formal renderings:

Carmine	Yellow Ochre	Cobalt
Light Red	Gamboge	Ultramarine Blue
Vermilion	Emerald Green	Payne's Grey
	Chinese White	(occasionally)

This is the palette of Professor Paul Phillipe Cret of Philadelphia, one of the most distinguished aquarellists in the profession. He says: "For water color, I use

Light Red or	Chrome Yellow #1	Cerulean Blue
Indian Red	Chrome Yellow #4	Cobalt Blue
Vermilion	Yellow Lake	French Blue
Carmine	Yellow Ochre	Prussian Blue
Raw Sienna	Emerald Green	Van Dyke Brown
Burnt Sienna	Veronese Green	Sepia

"This is not absolutely 'ne varietur'; I use occasionally one purple, Smalt Blue or what happens to be around and not too dry.

"For architectural rendering in color I have no special range of pigments, using part of the group above according to the color scheme selected.

"I have used either pure India Ink or a mixture of Ivory Black and Raw Sienna most frequently."

The extraordinary ability of Otto R. Eggers and his reputation as one of the greatest draughtsmen of modern times make the colors he uses of unusual interest to the student. I give his own words:

"I use all Winsor & Newton tube colors as follows:

Light Red	Cadmium Orange	New Blue
Warm Sepia	Chrome Orange	Neutral Tint
Brown Pink	Chrome Yellow	Mauve
Chinese White	Raw Sienna	Ivory Black
	Sap Green	

"For outdoor sketching I use those mentioned but never Black, and Chinese White very rarely.

"I may add that wherever possible I substitute Raw Sienna for Brown Pink, especially for outdoor work."

Birch Burdette Long, whose name is known in every architectural household through his perspective renderings, but who does not indulge in formal work, makes use of

Crimson Lake	Cadmium Pale	Antwerp Blue
Venetian Red	Cadmium Orange	New Blue
Vermilion	Chinese White	Indigo
	Burnt Sienna	

For special purposes:

Aureolin Yellow	Viridian Green
Raw Sienna	Hooker's Green
Raw Umber	Ivory Black

Tempera:

Zinnobar Green (light)
Zinnobar Green (dark)
Ultramarine Blue (dark)

PLATE 17   BY HUBERT G. RIPLEY

This drawing is made in body color on grey paper and the pencil drawing is made to play
a part in giving it vigor. Observe the unerring skill in the choice of subject and point of
view and the way the big darks and lights are massed.

Frank Hazell's sketches of architecture are as delightful as his landscapes. He uses transparent and body color in the same drawing. This is the palette with which he gets such extraordinary brilliancy:

Alizarin Crimson	Ultramarine or French Blue
Vermilion (a little)	Cobalt Blue
Chinese White	Cadmium Orange
Cadmium Yellow (medium)	Hooker's Green (light)
Yellow Ochre	Hooker's Green (dark)

Hubert G. Ripley of Boston, whose beautiful work is not sufficiently well known outside the Hub, uses the following:

For free work in water color and for architectural rendering in full color:

Alizarin Crimson	Aurora Yellow	Prussian Blue
Rose Madder	Lemon Yellow	Cerulean Blue
Orange Vermilion	Yellow Carmine	French Blue
	Chinese White	
	Mauve	

This he simplifies for rapid sketching to

Alizarin Crimson	French Blue
Aurora Yellow	Chinese White

In formal academic rendering he uses ground India Ink as a base with Aurora and Lemon Yellow, French Blue, Alizarin Crimson and Mauve as toning agents.

He says: "The manipulation of the colors after they are applied and thoroughly dry on the drawing changes greatly the effect of the finished work,—blotting out with light washes of water, scrubbing down; and softening with a bristle brush here and there; glazing over, and many other methods produce an infinite variety of effects at will.

"Sometimes a very good tone may be made by starting in with a soft pencil, making almost the full rendering; going over it with India Ink, jet black in spots, dragging a dry brush over in places; then applying washes of mauve and cramoisie; blotting out, scrubbing down; glazing; and finally waxing and polishing with a woolen rag, or an old pair of woolen socks."

VIII

FULL COLOR AND FREE SKETCHING

When we paint, we architects are, as a class, dogged by our technical knowledge, and cursed with a professional conscience which will permit of no deviation from the truth. Our training as architects unfits us for the point of view of the painter. When we sketch buildings at home or abroad we make documents of them. We know that a certain molding up there has just such a profile, and that capital just such decoration, and we try to combine the virtues of a measured drawing and of a water color by Sargent or Walcott. But the painter can beat us hollow when it comes to painting architecture. He knows little and cares less about mouldings and details of ornament. Where to us they tell a lot of things we oughtn't to know when we are painting, to him they are masses and bands and spots of light and shade. We work under the constant handicap of our technical knowledge of form. For that reason it is better, I think, when we go a-painting to sketch things with the actual forms of which we are not so familiar—ships and things along the waterfront, trees and rocks and sand and clouds. We can then see or learn to see objects with an unprejudiced eye and this will react later upon our vision of architectural form; for it will teach us not merely to make better sketches of architecture but to do better architecture because we have learned to think in the larger terms of light and shade and mass.

There are two principal aims in making a sketch; they cannot well be combined and so the best policy is to keep them quite distinct in your mind when you sit down. One is to sketch for your own education, for practise in rendering the exact truth, the absolute facts of the scene before you without special reference to their harmony—I mean of course such facts as you select from the scene before you—to get their color as seen under the lighting of the moment, the atmosphere of the hour. The other is to make a corking good sketch that people will admire and cause them to wag their heads and tell other people you are a clever fellow; and such a sketch has nothing to do with the truth of the matter; if a mass doesn't arrange itself well with other masses, move it over; if the color is not harmonious, make it so; recompose the whole thing, if you like, using what you see merely as a motif, in form and color. You are not seeking facts, you are on a quest for beauty and the sole justification of a rearrangement, suppression or creation of facts is that you produce something more beautiful thereby.

So also there are well marked distinctions between painting landscape and architecture from Nature out of doors, making a drawing of some building of our own in which we wish to bring out facts or just making this clever sketch—differences in aim and intention. Most of our foreign sketching must naturally, if we are serious students of our art, be in the direction of making accurate transcripts of what we most like. When we go abroad we are irresistibly impelled to set down on paper our impressions of the buildings or compositions which impress us. They seem wonderfully beautiful, too beautiful to try to improve upon, and so we humbly try to render that beauty as truly and faithfully as we can. And tone by tone and value by value, shadow by shadow, and light by wonderful light we do our best. The same is usually

PLATE 18   BY JULES GUÉRIN

This drawing illustrates admirably the interest with which an artist of vision can invest an
essentially commonplace and restless design by presenting it in an unusual aspect. Look at it
upside down also.

true of sketching landscape from Nature. As with an architectural subject, we choose our moment, when the light is favorable to our vision of it, when it is enveloped in atmosphere or sparkling in sunshine or gleaming softly under the moon. But in the type of sketch referred to above where the subject is merely a peg to hang an effect upon and to do just as we please with, irrespective and regardless of the truth of things, our fancy is our only guide. We tell the purists who preach against the iniquity of using body color and transparent color in the same drawing to go hang—and take grey paper or buff paper or any tone we like and transparent color and Chinese White and Mr. Ripley's old pair of woolen socks and have the time of our lives —frequently making our very best sketches.

Choice of Subject and Point of View. Choosing not merely the point of view but the aspect of a subject has everything to do with the interest and success of the sketch because these are constructive and fundamental. And beyond these still lies the choice of the subject. Some men always seem to select with unerring taste and judgment not merely the most distinguished subjects but the most distinguished and interesting point of view and their most beguiling aspects. Much of this is of course inborn and instinctive, but the judgment and taste may be trained by observation, study and comparison. Some men seem instinctively to pick out stupid subjects, lighted in stupid ways. Keep looking at sketches by the best men and dissect and analyze their charm. As a special case in point refer to Plate No. 19, a sketch by Hubert Ripley, and observe how he chose the most interesting spot, to an inch, from which to make his sketch. Note how Jules Guérin invariably selects the distinguished point of view and aspect of a distinguished subject. (See Plate No. 18 and frontispiece.)

Composition.   In any sketch the choice of the point of view is the most important factor, the time of day second and the kind of day third.   The first will give you your composition of line and mass, the second your composition of light and shade, the next your values and key.

Key.   I have deferred the definition of "key" till now because while it is perfectly applicable to monotone renderings, it has a closer relation to a painting in color.   Value being the *quantity* of light in a tone, Color being the *quality* of light in a tone, "Key" is the *pitch* of the drawing or painting itself.   This may be most clearly explained by an example.   A painting of starlight would have very little light in it; therefore while the values in it must be relatively right, each to each, they would be said to be "low" and the pitch of the painting as a whole (its "key") would also be low.   Conversely both the values and the key of a picture of blinding sunlight would be "high."   Which leads us to the postulate that the term "Values" applies to details and their relations to each other, and that "Key" applies to the drawing or painting as a whole.

Appliances.   In an office it may be assumed that we are provided with proper appliances for our work, blotters at hand, plenty of godets and tumblers and bowls.   Even at home the pantry may be levied upon and finger bowls and saucers and plates requisitioned and in both places there will be lots of running water.   For the field, however, we must make careful provision.   Whether for outdoors or indoors I believe in a folding metallic white-enameled palette with stalls for the colors on one of its halves.   Some kinds have depressed places in one of the

PLATE 19   BY HUBERT G. RIPLEY

Illustrating the choice of a point of view. Observe the interesting relation of the
cornice to the wall, indicating the width of the pavilion. (See p. 135.) This reproduction does scant justice to the values of the drawing, which it was apparently
impossible to photograph correctly. It is done in body color on yellowish paper
which shows through the blue sky, the Chinese White wash run over the architectural
forms, and the purple shadows. The ground beyond the steps is rich yellow and the
trees vivid green with yellow lights.

halves which will hold quite a lot of wash for skies and such. Somehow, though perhaps it is a matter of habit, you feel more as though you were painting when your thumb is in the hole in the palette and you have partially mastered the trick of keeping it level so that the washes don't run off on to your trousers. With such a palette, you carry your surplus supply of colors in a pocket or somewhere. Your precious brushes should be in a case, strapped with an elastic band to a flat cardboard so that they may not be injured. A perfect water bottle has still to be invented—try some and take the one you hate least. An army canteen is good. I find an old whisky flask pretty good except for a faint disturbing aroma which clings about the cork. There are good sketching stools and easels to be had. It isn't a bad thing to have indoor and outdoor conditions alike, so far as one can. It makes, by force of habit, for unconsciousness of appliances and inconveniences. When you first go out into the field after a long period of ease and luxury indoors—the luxury of plenty of water, places to lay things down, no wind, no dust, no mosquitoes, no horseflies—you go nearly crazy and your mind is so taken up with keeping your palette level and protecting yourself against dear old Nature that it is hardly tranquil enough for a good sketch. Be just as comfortable as you can indoors or out. If your legs are all cramped up with an uncomfortable seat, or if you think you'll get along without a seat and take the ground and find yourself sitting in a puddle or on an iceberg, you can't paint.

Mounted Paper. Believing as I do in a plane surface to work upon, I advocate mounting the paper solid on cardboard with another piece (of common paper) mounted on the back to counteract the pull and keep the board flat. Both indoors and outdoors it is also possible for those who like to work on wet paper to take a piece of glass (a picture glass, frame and all, if you please), soak your paper till it is limp and lay it on the glass. It will keep very wet for a long time and of course perfectly flat; also of course the drawing must be made on the paper before it is wet. With a little practise the most ripping things may be done. The color has to be put on much stronger than you would use if you were working on dry paper because it soaks in so much. As the paper dries, the portions requiring more definition are put in, until you reach the crisp accents when the paper is almost dry. (Plate No. 20.)

Setting the Palette. After you have made the drawing you will "set your palette" which means squeezing out your tube colors in a certain sequence or arranging your pans in that order. There are various ways of doing it and every man swears by his own. It seems simple and logical to follow the sequence in the spectrum and this is always easy to remember. Starting at the left, Red, Orange, Yellow, Green, Green Blue, Blue, Violet. If I have Payne's Grey I put it last, on the right, and Chinese White on the extreme left. This would also mean that if you had three Blues, for instance, on your palette, Cyanine Blue would go in the Green Blue space, Cobalt in the Blue space, French Blue next to the Violet space. But heaven forbid that you should go forth to sketch with any such array of colors as this would suggest. With one Red, one Yellow, one Blue and Chinese White, you'll come back with a simpler, stronger, cleaner sketch than you ever made before and probably one in key. The reason for an habitual arrangement of your colors is that presently your brush goes to the color you want instinctively

PLATE 20   BY THE AUTHOR

To illustrate working on wet paper laid on a sheet of glass. (See p. 138.) The general tones are
put on first, and as the paper dries the parts requiring more definition are put in, and the crisp
accents when the paper is almost dry. The color has to be put on much stronger than usual
because it soaks in; and shadow washes, for example, put on very wet paper have to be pushed
back into place with the brush to keep them from spreading too much and losing all definition.

as the fingers of a pianist or a typist find the keys without process of thought.

Use of Black.   Black is not mentioned here because it has no place, in my opinion, in work in full color except in decoration.   Black is the negation of color.   If you look carefully enough and long enough at something in Nature which seems on a cursory view to be black you will discover that it isn't black at all but dark grey or brown or violet.   There is no black in Nature and one of the marked differences between the older and the new schools of painting is in the banishment of black from the palette by the latter.

Brushes.   A brand-new sharply pointed brush is for most purposes in free sketching a deterrent of success; for certain details it is indispensable, but for most uses one somewhat blunted is preferable.   Flat bristle brushes have their merits and should be tried out to determine their virtues and limitations.   A sketch made with flat brushes of different sizes and widths may be given a very distinctive quality by the character of the brush strokes.

Papers.   As to paper, anything you like is the thing for you —smooth Whatman, rough and extra rough Whatman, Harding paper (a buff paper with a strong diagonal grain and quite absorbent and in this year of grace 1921 hard to get), English tinted crayon paper (*not* the smooth side), French "Torchon" paper, charcoal paper.   In using tinted or colored paper you must bear in mind that the darker it is, the furthest removed from white, the more it will lower the value of every tone.   As I have said, in water color painting the white of white paper is counted upon to take the place of the white pigment used in oil painting. Therefore the tone of the paper modifies any transparent wash to a tremendous extent and Chinese White must frequently be resorted to in order to make a light wash opaque enough to cover the paper and prevent it from changing the tone of the wash.

F. Hopkinson Smith used to have a lot of paper of different tones with him from which he selected that one which was nearest to the general tone of the scene, and with a few modifications of this tone made here with transparent, there with opaque washes and a few touches of local color, he produced very clever and beautiful sketches. They weren't very true, the sunlight in them rarely seemed like real sunshine, but they were very charming nevertheless.

Howard Greenley makes very clever sketches by choosing a darkish paper and working on it in body color, leaving the color of the paper to represent the shadows, the stone joints and the like.

Methods. As to the actual painting, the putting on of the color, that cannot be taught or described in a book. I can only give a hint here and there. I learned by hints picked up here and there from this man and that. Study everybody and learn something from each and presently your work will begin to take on a personal accent. Study Fortuny, Harpignies, Whistler, Sargent, Brangwyn, Maris, Israels, Walcott, Guérin, Parrish, Dodge McKnight, Frank Hazell, Herman Murphy. When Robert Louis Stevenson was learning to write he deliberately set himself the task of imitating as closely as he could the styles of various masters of English, rendering a given theme or sentence as each of them would have done. The result was a style so personal that one has but to hear a sentence by Stevenson with the eyes closed to recognize it instantly. It is the best sort of practise to copy provided you copy the work of several, the more

PLATE 21   BY OTTO R. EGGERS

Façade of St. Peters in Rome. Illustrating an interesting point of view and an admirable
rendition of textures.

widely divergent in method and style the better. The list of men just given indicates a range wide enough for any one.

Unless you are making a documentary sort of sketch it is the worst kind of mistake to make an elaborate pencil outline drawing first. If you do you get a colored drawing. The moment you make a careful line sketch the tendency is to tighten up when you come to the color. A few of the principal lines to define the big masses, the location of important darks and the rest of the drawing done entirely with the brush. Painters in fact often draw entirely with the brush in pale blue or red—not a bad idea for the architect to adopt.

Beginning to Paint. I think it is usually best to put your sky in first, frequently carrying it down over the whole drawing, running it out to water and blotting it up where you don't want it. This makes sure that it is carried down behind the trees and so on. Then the far distance, distance, middle distance and foreground in this order, to ensure measures of value as in formal rendering.

Sometimes you have to model a good deal as you go, especially in a diffused light without any real shadows, but the usual procedure is to put on the shadows last, of which, naturally, the most important are the first to be done.

But it is hard to follow any rule. Each subject has its own exigencies and requirements, and must be carefully analyzed for values, color masses and modulation before beginning to paint in order to determine the steps to take and the proper sequence of those steps. This is of course chiefly applicable to work in transparent as distinguished from body color; in body color you may cover up lots of early mistakes.

It is well to take both blotter and sponge with you when you go out. Always wet the sponge before you go, for water is usually precious in the field. And if you make a bad start just sponge it out at once and start afresh.

It is not necessary to use the point of the brush always. In breaking one color over another it is often more effective to use the side. For the rendition of some effects, such as deep grass, not merely should the point be used but the brush should be held by the extreme end of the handle. At other times it should be firmly grasped and used like a lead pencil. By all of which I mean to indicate that you should not stand on ceremony with your tools or materials. For some parts of a water color drawing it may be held nearly vertical on an easel—but there is no law of God or man which debars you from holding it flat on your knees or putting it on the ground if by so doing you can get what you want. Work upside down if you like, inverting yourself or your drawing as most convenient. And don't let any one tell you that this or that method is not "legitimate" or "fair."

Scrubbing. You will see that the Dutch painters often scrub the paper, not merely to remove hard edges here and there but to produce certain effects of light in cloudy skies and elsewhere. In view of their lovely results it is evident that when you wish you may scrub the paper all you please—but be sure your result is lovely.

Textures. Some effects of texture may best be rendered by a general wash varied in tone and laid very wet. Then when perfectly dry, drag color over it where you want it with a pretty dry brush.

Manipulation. Color, particularly deposing color, has to be manipulated to get the most out of its possibilities. The beginner is apt to work too quickly and not give it a chance to settle

PLATE 22   BY ERNEST PEIXOTTO

A painter's chief concern is with the big elements of a composition; an architect is usually obsessed by detail. This drawing exhibits the point of view of a distinguished painter and illustrator.

out. Suppose we have a big blank wall in which there is a considerable variety of tone, red running into yellow or merging into grey or violet in places. To get quality and a sense of texture and of the vibration of light, mix up some red, some yellow and some violet of the right values and have them ready; then begin at the top and pull the color slowly, working the brush sometimes from right to left, sometimes from left to right, sometimes diagonally in either direction, sometimes vertically, sometimes fast, sometimes slow, and taking up the colors you need as you come to them, blending them together where they need it, keeping them apart when necessary; now and then you'll need to take water to lighten up a tone—but be sure you take up no more than you require to lighten the tone or you'll get a fan or a run-back—"All parts of the wash equally wet" applies in free as in formal rendering. By this process you arrange the tiny particles of pigment in different relative positions, giving variety to the same tone by the mere variety in handling. This is of course a mere hint at the possibilities of manipulation. Water color work is not merely laying perfect flat washes nor evenly and perfectly graded washes, but also giving quality to a wash by the way it is modulated by handling—and to the expert eye this is one of the marks of the adept or of the novice.

Broadly speaking, there are two systems by which washes in full color may be laid—particularly large washes. One is by mixing the various pigments together and floating them on in one wash. The other way is to float one color over another. They both require considerable skill. Great judgment is required in mixing the mixed wash and great lightness of hand in laying the colors singly. As has been frequently observed, it is apt to give a wash containing heavy color a muddy appearance if the little particles of pigment are disturbed and disarranged. For that reason, in building up a compound tone with individual washes, it is well to lay the washes of the lighter pigments first. For example, if you wish to lay a Violet, put on a wash of Carmine first and over that float Cobalt or Ultramarine. When well done this individual-wash method has great beauty.

Spraying on Full Color. For sprayed washes put on by air-brush or atomizer in full color, it is by all odds the best way to build up the tone instead of mixing red and blue together to make a Violet and then spraying on the mixture. It is far more beautiful to spray on the separate colors. The tiny spots of each pigment fall side by side on the paper and the eye blends them.

* * *

So much for method and methods; but beyond these lies that inner vision without which all work however skilfully done is empty and soulless.

INDEX

A

	PAGE
Accessory Trees and Shrubs	88
Accuracy in Plans	100, 101
Acropolis	84
Aerial Photographs	100
Agents, Pigments as Toning	29, 30
Alcohol, Diluting with	49
Alcohol Spray	49
Alteneder Ruling Pens	20
Alternate Method of Laying a Sky Wash	43
Alum, Use of	23
Aims in Sketching	133
Air Brush	48, 113
" " Skies	47
" " Washes, Repairing Defects in	42
" " or Atomizer, Unifying Tone with	113
Analysis of Color Masses and their Modulation	141
" " Subject	141
Antiquarian Paper	4
Appliances	136
Arrangement of Colors, Habitual	138
"Art" Gum	17, 22, 108
Atomizer Skies	47
" or Air Brush, Unifying Tone with	113
Atomizers	48, 113
Author's Palette	126

B

	PAGE
"Background" vs. Sky	35
Backgrounds, Warm and Cold	83
Back shades	77
Back Shadows, Drawing	63, 69
" " and Piquage	76
Balance, Reversal for	62, 63
Beginning to Paint	141
"Biting in" a line	18, 75
Black, Use of	139
Blaisdell Pencil	81
Block Plans	113
Blots, Removing	51
Blotters	10, 141
" and their Uses	28, 29
Board, Drawing	3
Board, Tilting the Drawing	50

	PAGE
Body Color	82, 128
Brangwyn, Frank	140
Brickwork, Piquage of	79
Brilliancy by Contrasts	44, 70
" Preserving	44
Brilliant Poché	104, 105
Bristle Brushes, Flat and Chinese	139
Broad Lines	100, 106
Brown, to make	125
Brush Case	137
" Drawing with the	141
" Loading the	38
" The Point of the	142
" The Side of the	142
" Selecting a	26
Brushes, Air	48
" Camels' Hair	26
" Care of	27
" Chinese Bristle	27
" Flat Hair or Bristle	139
" Red Sable	25
" Winsor & Newton's	25
Building assumed to be rendered, Description of	17, 34
Building up from light to dark	36
" " Gradations	66
" " Plane Values	57
" " Values	96

C

Camels' Hair Brushes	26
Carbonaceous Pigments	123
" Washes	41, 110
Care of Brushes	27
" " Stick of Ink	28
Carrying the Wash Out	54
Case, Brush	137
Casserole, Use of	23
Casting Shadows	24
Ceiling Indication	105
" Solids, Shadows of	93
Character in Furnishing, Expression of	107
Charcoal Paper	139
Charrette	22
Charrette, En	16
Chifflot	21
Chinese Bristle Brushes	27
" Ink	27
Choice of Subject and Point of View	135
Circulation, Grey	105
" Tone of	105
" White	105
Clean Hands	11
Cleaning, "Dry"	22
Cleaning off	22
Cleanliness	11, 108
" again	29

PAGE

Cloth-backed Paper 6
Cloud Shadows 113
Coarsening Freehand Pens.. 20
Cold Backgrounds, Warm and 83
Cold and Warm Lines.. 101
   "   "   "   Tones, Opposing 84
   " -Pressed Whatman Paper 4
   " to Warm and Vice Versa, Grading from....................... 88
Colonnade Shadows 70
Color, Body 82, 128
   "   Drawing in Quarter, Half and Three-quarter 83
   "   Full 133
   "   Habitual Arrangement of.................................... 138
   "   "Lifting" of 87, 91
   "   Local 52
   "   Manipulation of 142
   "   Masses and Their Modulation, Analysis of.................. 141
   "   Piquage in 89
   "   Powders 128
   "   Saucer (godet) 29
   "   Spraying on in Full 144
Colors, Beware of old dry... 123
   "   Fugitive 118, 119
   "   Pan 116
   "   Primary 89, 124
   "   Secondary 89
   "   Tertiary 89
   "   Tube 116
Column Shades and Shadows... 73
Combined Gradations 45
Common Sense in Indication.. 104
Complicated Shadows 24
Composition 136
Compound Tone by Individual Washes.................................... 144
Concentration of Interest in Plan.................................... 113
   "   " Light and Dark in Plans.............................. 111
Conditions, Indoor and Outdoor....................................... 137
Construction Lines for Shadows....................................... 24
"Consuming" the Line.. 19
Conté Crayon 81
Contrast, Law of.. 111
   "   Reversing Values for 53
Contrasts, Brilliancy by...44, 70
Convention xv
   "   vs. Realism 46
Conventional Indications 109
Cooling Ink 17
Copying 140
Cornice Shadow, Sharp Gradation in.................................... 68
   "   Shadows 66, 86
   "   " Minor Planes in (Diagram)...........................55, 67
Crayon Paper, English and Tinted...................................... 139
Cret, Paul Philippe..84, 98
   "   "   Working Palette of 129
Crossing Lines 103
Crow-quill Pens 80
Curved Surfaces, Illumination of...................................... 57
Cyma Shades, Gradation of... 96

PAGE

D

Damp Weather 50
Dampening the Drawing.. 37
Dark Horizons 45
   " Lines 19
Darkening up 81
Darks and Lights, Principal.. 65
Defects in Airbrush Washes, Repairing.. 42
   " Repairing 41
Demi-poché 101
Deposing Pigments 116
Description of Building assumed to be rendered.............................17, 34
   " " Monotone and Monochrome............................ 31
D'Espouy 18, 20, 64, 94, 95
Details, Light Edges in.. 97
   " Rendering of 94
   " Textures in 99
Diluting Ink 17
   " with Alcohol 49
Diminishing Glass 69
Discipline xvi
Distances 45
Division of Washes.. 33
Drawing at Small Scale, Simplification of..................................... 13
   " Back Shadows 69
   " Dampening the 37
   " of Plan, Freedom in 101
   " with the Brush 141
   " Rendering Detail 94
   " Board 3
   " " Tilting the 50
Drawings in Quarter, Half and Three-quarter Color............................ 83
   " Shade-line 21
"Dry-cleaning" 22
Dull Poché 103

E

Easels 137
Edges in Details, Light... 97
   " Mending 40
   " of a Wash, Freshening up the 38
Edifices de Rome Moderne—Letarouilly... 107
Eggers, Otto R., Working Palette of... 129
Eggshell Paper 4
Electric Fan, Use of...10, 23
Eliminating Spots and Streaks...41, 42
En Charrette 16
English Crayon Paper.. 139
Ensemble 101
Entourage 100
   " and Tree Masses Generally 108
Envois of the Grand Prix Men.. 18
Erasures 14
Erechtheion 84
Evaporation of Ink, Preventing the... 28
Experimenting 87

PAGE

Expression of Character in Furnishing.. 107
Extra Rough Whatman Paper...139

F

Fan, Use of Electric...10, 23
"Fans" or "run-backs"...5, 29, 50, 143
Field, Sponge for the...141, 142
Final Paper, Transferring Studies to... 12
Flat Hair and Bristle Brushes..139
Floor Indication 105
Foliage 82
    "   Use of Sponge for 112
Following a Line... 38
Foregrounds, Perspective 46
Fortuny 140
Free Sketching 133
Freedom in Drawing of Plan...101
Free-hand Pens 20
    "   "   Coarsening and Sharpening of.................................... 20
Freshening up Edges of a Wash.. 38
"Frothing" 15
Frotter 15
Fugitive Colors 118, 119
Full Color 133
    "   Spraying on in...144
Furnishing a Plan..105, 106
    "   "   Use of Washes in.......................................107
    "   Expression of Character in...................................107
Furniture 105

G

Garnier, Tony 102
Gillott's Pens 20
Glass, Diminishing 69
    "   Painting on 137, 138
Glazing Method, The.. 90
Godefroy 65
Godet (Color Saucer)... 29
Goodhue, Bertram G..47, 104
Gouache 128
Gradation in Plans...110
    "   of Cyma Shades... 96
    "   " Steps... 70
    "   " Windows 71
Gradations, Building up.. 66
    "   Combined 45
    "   Reversing 62
Grading a Wash from Light to Dark and Vice Versa................................... 37
    "   from Cold to Warm and Vice Versa............................... 88
    "   Modillion Shadows 69
    "   of Plane Washes 62
    "   Plane Washes Upwards 62
    "   Small Washes 71
Grand Prix Men...94, 95, 96
    "   " Envois of the..................................... 18
Graphite 11, 15

PAGE

Green Rubber 22
Greenley, Howard 140
Grey Circulation 105
" To make 125
Greys of Plan 105
Grinding or Rubbing up India Ink...................................... 28
Grinding Saucer, Slate...28, 104
Guérin, Jules 81, 115, 116, 120, 122, 135, 140
" " Working Palette of.. 129

H

Habitual Arrangement of Colors.. 138
Hair Line 103
Handling in Plans, Subtlety of.. 108
Hands, Clean 11
Harding Paper 139
Harmony 83, 101
Harpignies 140
Hatching 41
Hatfield's Colors 116
Hazell, Frank 140
" " Working Palette of... 131
Heavy Pigments 116
" " Settling out of.. 118
Hedges 108
Higgins' Ink 17, 103, 104
" Paste 5
High and Low Key or Pitch... 136
Hopeless Stage, The... 51
Horizons, Dark 45
Horizontal Working 143
Hot Pressed Whatman Paper... 4

I

Illumination of Curved Surfaces....................................... 57
" " Planes, Relative 55
Importance of Program xiii
India Ink 22, 28, 32
" " "Rubbing up" or "Grinding" of................................ 28
" " Rendering and Pure Color, Intermediate step between.......... 85
Indication, Ceiling and Floor... 105
" Common Sense in 104
Indications, Conventional 109
Individual vs. Mixed Washes... 143
" Washes, Compound Tone by... 144
Indoor Conditions 137
Indoor and Outdoor Scale in Plan...................................... 107
Ink, Care of Stick of... 28
" Chinese 27
" Cooling or Warming..17, 18
" Diluting 17
" Higgins' 17, 103, 104
" India 27, 28, 32
" Keeping 28
" Preventing the Evaporation of.................................... 28
" Straining 28

	PAGE
Ink, Toning the	17
Inking in of Plan	103
"　" Shadows	24
Inner Vision	24
Interest concentrated in Plan	113
Intermediate or Subordinate Planes	58
"　Step between India Ink Rendering and Pure Color	83
Israels	136

J

Joining Sheets (of paper)	5
Joint Lines	21
Juxtaposition of Varied Tones	89

K

Keeping Ink	28
Keeping the Wash evenly wet	38, 73
Key	136
"　High and Low	136
"　Preservation of	83, 84

L

Larger Scale, Studies at	13
Law of Contrast	111
Laying Sky Washes	36, 37
"Legitimate" Methods	142
Letarouilly's Edifices de Rome Moderne	107
"Lifting" of Color	87, 91
Light and Dark in Plans, Concentration of	111
"　Edges in Details	97
"　Lines	100
"　Reflected	58
"　(Color), Quality of	31, 136
"　(Value), Quantity of	31, 136
"　to Dark, Building up from	36
"　"　"　or Vice Versa, Grading a Wash from	37
Lightening up	17
Lights and Darks, Principal	65
Lightweight Pigments	116
Line and its Quality, The	18
"　"Biting in" a	18, 75
"　"Consuming" the	19
"　Following a	38
"　Hair	103
"　Drawings, Shade-	21
"　Watertable	110
"　Working	12
Lines, Broad and Soft	20, 100, 106
"　Cold and Warm	101
"　Crossing	103
"　Dark	19
"　for shadows, Construction	24
"　Joint	21
"　Light	19, 100
"　Piquage by	79
"　Speed in Drawing	18

PAGE

Lines, Thick 18
  "   Thin 18
  "   Window (in plans) 103, 104
  "   Wiry 18, 106
  "   vs. Planes 19
Loading the Brush... 38
Local Color 52
Long, Birch Burdette, Working Palette of.................................... 130
Low Key or Pitch.. 136
Luminosity 41
Luminous Washes 41

M

McGoodwin's Shades and Shadows... 25
McKnight, Dodge 140
Main Cornice Shadows... 86
Manipulation of Color... 142
  "   Speed of 84
Maris 140
Meagreness 105, 109
Medaille des Concours... 100
Mending Edges 40
Method of Laying a Sky Wash, Alternate...................................... 43
  "   The Glazing 90
Methods, "Legitimate" 142
  "   in Sketching 140
  "   of Grading Small Washes... 71
Metal Work and Windows, Piquage of.. 79
Minor Plane Values.. 65
  "   Planes in Cornice Shadows (Diagram)...........................55, 67
Mixed vs. Individual Washes... 143
Modillion Shadows, Grading.. 69
Monochrome and Monotone, Definition of...................................... 31
Monotone 31, 83
  "   and Monochrome, Definitions of.................................... 31
Mounted Paper 137
Mounting of Paper...5, 7
Mother Wash, The...32, 85
Murphy, Herman 140

O

Old dry colors, Beware of.. 123
  "   seasoned paper best... 27
Opaque Pigments 116
Openings, Warm or Cold Tones in...87, 88
Opposing Cold and Warm Tones.. 84
Ornament, Shadows of.. 75
Outdoor and Indoor Scale in Plan... 107
  "   Conditions 137
Outlining Poché 103, 104

P

Pace in Running Washes... 123
Paint, Beginning to.. 141

PAGE

Painting on Glass..137, 138
    " Scrubbing the Paper in Sketching or....................... 142
Pale Lines 19
Palette, Establishing a Working.................................. 126
    " Folding 136
    " of Author 26
    " " Paul P. Cret 129
    " " Otto R. Eggers 129, 130
    " " Jules Guérin...................................... 129
    " " Frank Hazell 131
    " " Birch Burdette Long 130
    " " Hubert G. Ripley 131
    " Setting the 138
Pan Colors 116
Paper, Antiquarian 4
    " Blotting 28
    " Charcoal 139
    " Cloth-backed 6
    " Eggshell 4
    " English Crayon 139
    " for Sketches 139
    " Harding 139
    " Joining Sheets of..................................... 5
    " Lightweight 4
    " Mounted 137
    " Mounting of 5, 7
    " Old seasoned, Best 7
    " Preserving the Surface of............................. 14
    " Protecting the 14
    " Roll 4, 5
    " Selection of 7
    " Steinbach 4
    " Thin 4
    " Tinted Crayon 139
    " Torchon 139
    " Transfer 16
    " Use of Alum for re-calendering the 23
    " Whatman Cold Pressed 4
    " " Hot " 4
    " " Extra Rough 139
    " " Roll 4
    " " Rough 139
    " " Smooth 139
Parrish, Maxfield 115, 140
Parthenon 84
Passing Plane Washes... 54
Paste, Higgins' 5
Pattern 102
Pen Shadows, Ruling-... 75
Pencil, Blaisdell 81
Penciling in 14
    " " a Plan 103
Pens, Alteneder's Ruling... 20
    " Coarsening and Sharpening Freehand................... 20
    " Crow-quill 20
    " Freehand 20
    " Gillot's 20
    " Ruling 20, 75

	PAGE
Penumbra	98
Permanence of Pigments	117
Perspective Foregrounds	46
Perspective in Plan, Trees in	111
Perspectives	90
Photographs, Aerial (footnote)	100
Pigments as Toning Agents	29
" Carbonaceous	123
" Deposing	116
" Heavy	116
" Lightweight	116
" Opaque	116
" Permanence of	117
" Properties of	84, 116
" Settling out of heavy	118
" Transparent	89, 116
Piquage	17, 32, 62, 70, 78, 97
" and Back Shadows	76
" by Lines	79
" in Color	89
" of Brickwork	79
" " Stonework	78
" " Windows and Metal Work	79
" Texture by	79
" Use of the Rubber in	80
Piquer	17, 89
Pitch	138
Pitches of Platforms, etc., Whites in	12
Plan, Concentration of Interest in a	113
" Crossing Lines in	103
" Freedom in Drawing of	101
" Furnishing a	106
" Indoor and Outdoor Scale in	107
" Inking in of a	103
" in Rendering, Simplification of	109
" Penciling in of a	103
" Preliminary Study of Values in a	109
" Shadows	112
" Subtlety of Handling in	108
" The Greys of a	105
" Third Dimension in	102
" Trees in Perspective in a	111
" Use of Washes in Furnishing a	107
" Washes in	110
Plans, Accuracy in	100, 101
" Block	113
" Concentration of Light and Dark in	111
" Gradation of	110
" Meagreness in	105
" Rendering of	100
" Window Lines in	104
Plane Values	52, 57
" " Minor	65
" Washes, Grading of	62
" " Passing	54
Planes in Line, Value of	17
" Intermediate or Subordinate	58
" Minor, in Cornice Shadows (Diagram)	55, 67

PAGE

Planes, Relative Illumination of 55
" vs. Lines 19
Planning out Washes.. 33
Plantations in Plans...108, 109
Platforms, etc., Whites in Pitches of................................. 12
Poché 101, 102
" Brilliant or Dull...104, 105
" Demi- 101
" Outlining 103, 104
Pocher 105
" Proper Time to... 105
Point of the Brush.. 142
" " View and Choice of Subject............................ 135
Powders, Color 128
Preliminary Steps 3
" Study of Values in Plans............................. 109
Preservation of Key..83, 84
Preserving Brilliancy 44
" the Surface of Paper.............................. 14
Preventing the Evaporation of Ink................................... 28
Primary Colors 89, 124
Principal Darks and Lights.. 65
Problem in Reflected Light, etc., Sections as....................... 93
Program, Importance of xiii
Properties of Pigments..84, 116
Propylæa 84
Protect Drawing, Shield to.. 14
Protecting the Paper.. 14
Puddles 10
Pure Monotone 31

Q

Quality of Light (Color)..31, 136
Quantity of Light (Value).......................................31, 136
Quality of Tone... 85
" The Line and its...................................... 18
Quarter Color, Half and Three-quarter Color, Drawings in........... 83

R

Rays, Spectrum 124
Realism vs. Convention.. 46
Re-calendering the Paper..23, 24
Red Sable Brushes...25, 26
Reflected Light 58
" Lights, Sections a problem in....................... 93
" Shades 77
" Shadows 63
Relative Illumination of Planes..................................... 55
Removing Blots 51
Rendering Details 94
" Plans 100
" Sections 93
" Simplification of plan in........................... 109
Repairing Defects 41
Reversal of gradations for balance.................................. 62
Reversing Values for Contrast....................................... 53

PAGE

Ripley, Hubert G..81, 84, 135
   "   "   " Working Palette of 131
Roll Paper 4, 5
Ross, Denman 31, 85
Rough Whatman Paper...139
Rubber Cement 47
Rubber, Use of the..80
Rubbers, Green and Ruby 22
Rubbing on 15
Rubbing up or Grinding India Ink 28
Ruby Rubber 22
Ruling-Pen Shadows 75
   " Pens 20
Runbacks or Fans..5, 6, 29, 30, 50, 143
Running Washes containing much Color..................................87
   "   "   Pace in 123
   "   "   too wet 39

S

Sanguine 16
Sargent, John S..135, 140
"Sauce" 108
Saucer, Color (godet) 29
   " Slate Grinding 28, 104
Scale, Indoor and Outdoor, in Plan....................................107
   " in Treatment 103
   " Simplification of Drawing at Small..............................13
   " Studies at Larger...13
   " Treatment in Relation to......................................103
Scrubbing the Paper in Sketching or Painting..........................142
Seats or Stools, Sketching 137
Secondary Colors 89
Sections, Problem in Reflected Light...................................89
   " Rendering of 93
Selecting a Brush..26
Selection of Paper..7
Sequence, Spectrum 126, 138
Setting the Palette...138
Settling-out of Heavy Pigments.......................................118
Shade-line Drawings 21
Shades and Shadows..65
   "   "   " Column 73
   "   "   " McGoodwin's 25
   " Back 77
   " Gradation of Cyma...96
   " Reflected 77
Shadows, Back 63, 69
   "   " and Piquage 76
   " Casting 24
   " Cloud 113
   " Colonnade 70
   " Complicated 24
   " Construction Lines for......................................24
   " Cornice 66
   " Grading Modillion 69
   " Inking in 24
   " Main Cornice 86
   " Minor Planes in Cornice..................................55, 67

PAGE

Shadows of Ceiling Solids 93
 " " Ornament 75
 "   Plan 112
 "   Reflected 63
 "   Ruling Pen 75
 "   Sharp Gradation in Cornice................................... 68
 "   Small 75
Sharp Gradation in Cornice Shadow................................. 68
Sharpening Freehand Pens.. 20
Sheets (of paper), Joining 5
Shield to Protect Drawing... 14
Shrubs and Trees, Accessory.. 88
Side of the Brush.. 142
Silhouettes 22
Simplification of Drawing at Small Scale............................ 13
 "   " Plan in Rendering.. 109
Sketches, Paper for.. 139
Sketching, Aims in... 133
 "   Free 133
 "   Methods in 140
 "   or Painting, Scrubbing the Paper in......................... 142
 "   Textures in 142
Skies, Air Brush 47
 " Atomizer 47
 " Sprayed 47
Sky Tones 35
 " vs. "Background" 35
 " Wash, Alternate Method of Laying a........................... 43
 " Washes 85, 86
 " " Laying 36, 37
Slate Grinding Saucer...28, 104
Small Scale, Simplification of Drawing at........................... 13
 " Shadows 75
 " Washes, Methods of Grading.................................... 71
Smith, F. Hopkinson.. 140
Smooth Whatman Paper... 139
Soft Lines 20, 100, 106
Solids, Shadows of Ceiling.. 93
Spectrum Rays 124
 " Sequence 126, 138
Speed in Drawing Lines.. 18
 " (or Pace) in Running Washes................................... 123
 " of Manipulation 84
Sponge, Face 23
 " for the Field..141, 142
 " " Foliage, Use of 112
Sponging down Washes...96, 99
 " off 23
Spots, Eliminating 41, 42
Spray, Alcohol 49
 " Washes, Templates for... 47
Sprayed Skies 47
Spraying on in Full Color... 144
Steinbach Paper 4
Steps, Gradation of... 70
Stevenson, Robert Louis... 140
Stick of Ink, Care of.. 28
Stippling 42

PAGE

Stone, Weathering of... 97
Stonework, Piquage of... 78
Straight-edge, Use of.. 5
Straining Ink... 28
Streaks, Eliminating 41, 42
Strips, Tick.. 12
Studies at Larger Scale... 13
    " to final paper, Transferring... 12
Study of Plan Values, Preliminary...108, 109
Subject and Point of View, Choice of... 135
    " Analysis of 141
Subtlety of Handling in Plan.. 108
Subordinate or Intermediate Planes.. 58
Surface of Paper, Preserving the.. 14
Surfaces, Illumination of Curved.. 57

T

Temperament 114
Templates for Spray Washes 47
Tertiary Colors 89
Texture by Piquage.. 79
Textures 81, 113
    " in Details 99
    " " Sketching 142
Thick Lines 18
Thin Lines 18
Thin and Lightweight Paper.. 4
Third Dimension in Plan... 102
Tick Strips 12
Tilting the Drawing Board... 50
Time to Pocher, Proper.. 105
Tinted Crayon Paper... 139
Tone, Quality of.. 85
    " of Circulation 105
    " Unified with Air Brush or Atomizer.. 113
    " Value of 85
Tones in Openings, Warm or Cold...87, 88
    " Juxtaposition of Varied 89
    " Opposing Cold and Warm.. 84
    " Sky 35
Toning Agents, Pigments as.. 29
    " the Ink 17
Torchon Paper 139
Transfer Paper 16
Transferring Studies to Final Paper... 12
Transparent Pigments 89, 116
    " Washes 41
Treatment in Relation to Scale.. 103
Tree Forms in Plan, Use of Sponge in.. 112
Tree Masses and Entourage Generally... 108
Trees 103
    " and Shrubs, Accessory.. 88
    " in Perspective in Plan.. 111
Tube Colors 116

U

Uniformity 34
Unifying Tone with Air Brush or Atomizer.. 113

PAGE

Unifying Washes 89
Use of Alum.. 23
" " Black 131
" " Blotters 28, 29
" " Casserole 23
" " Electric Fan 10, 23
" " the Rubber in Piquage... 80
" " Sponge for Foliage 112
" " Straight-edge 5
" " Washes in Furnishing Plan.. 107

V

Valley Forge Memorial... 98
Value of Tone... 85
Values 31
   " Building up 96
   " " " Plane 57
   " for contrast, Reversing.. 53
   " of Minor Planes... 65
   " " Planes 52
   " " Planes in Line.. 17
   " Preliminary Study of Plan... 109
Varied Tones, Juxtaposition of.. 89
View and Choice of Subject, Point of... 135
Villa Medici 94
Viollet-le-Duc 18

W

Walcott, William 133, 140
Ware, Professor William R.. 8
Warm and Cold Lines.. 101
   " " " Tones, Opposing 84
   " " " Backgrounds 83
   " " Vice Versa, Grading from Cold to.................................... 88
Warming Ink 17, 18
Wash, Alternate Method of Laying a Sky.. 43
   " cut to the end, Carrying the... 54
   " evenly wet, Keeping the... 38, 73
   " Freshening up the Edges of a.. 38
   " from Light to Dark and Vice Versa, Grading a......................... 37
   " Laying the Sky 36, 37
   " The Mother 32
Washes, Carbonaceous 41, 110
   " Compound Tone by Individual.. 144
   " containing much pigment, Running of.................................. 87
   " Division of 33
   " Grading of Plane... 62
   " in Plan 110
   " Laying Sky 36, 37
   " Luminous 41
   " Methods of Grading Small... 71
   " Pace or Speed in Running.. 123
   " Passing Plane 54
   " Planning out 33
   " Repairing Defects in Air Brush....................................... 42
   " too Wet, Running... 39

CPSIA information can be obtained at www.ICGtesting.com
Printed in the USA
LVOW091732201212

312633LV00008B/548/A